THEY LEFT D
. . . BUT THEY
THEIR MEMORIES BACK WITH THEM. AND SOMETHING MORE.

"The head nurse came back in and saw me in this luminous state, and she immediately recognized, I think, what had happened. I remember her just sort of kneeling down and crying, and she said to me later, 'This is holy ground.' "
—Alexandra, near-death survivor

"It had seemed that the boundary between life and death was at the top of the tunnel, where the light was. During the first two experiences, I felt sure that if I'd gone into that light, I wouldn't come back. Yet the third time, I was surrounded by it but I still came back."
—Olivia, three-time near-death survivor

These two women and the other "eyewitnesses" in this book found themselves in a place they never imagined existed . . . and face to face with a truth they would never forget. What they have to say is like a hand reaching out to us from the darkness, a portrayal of what awaits those . . .

WITHIN THE LIGHT

It was dark but not at all terrifying, and I was being pulled upward through a tunnel that became brighter and brighter. There was this light at the end of the tunnel. It was yellow/white, more white than gold, but indescribable and beautiful. It was a person but not a person; a god perhaps, but with no real shape. I took the person to be God, but God of all, not just one religion. It was a really pleasurable experience.
—Denise

And while I was up there it was like I was in this golden world, this incredible golden world filled with Christ light. I just felt I was part of it all, part of the whole, that this was where I belonged, that this was the truth. And there were all these beings, angels, angelic luminous beings and this feeling of total love. And the one thing I got when I was up there was that my task was to serve, that the only purpose for humans is to serve the planet and to live life absolutely to the fullest.
—Shana

Today I find that my whole life is always a prayer or a chat to God. I just talk to God like He's just there all the time. You know, if I need to know something I'll just sit down and I'll tune in and ask what I should be doing. It's always there, that information.
—Janet

Within the Light

Bantam Books by Cherie Sutherland Ph.D.

Reborn in the Light
Within the Light

Within the Light

Cherie Sutherland, PhD

BANTAM BOOKS

New York Toronto London Sydney Auckland

This edition contains the complete text of the original hardcover edition.
NOT ONE WORD HAS BEEN OMITTED.

WITHIN THE LIGHT

A Bantam Book

PUBLISHING HISTORY
First published in Australia and New Zealand in 1993 by Bantam
Bantam edition/June 1995

For information address: Bantam Books, 1540 Broadway, New York, NY 10036.

ISBN 0-553-56981-3

Published simultaneously in the United States and Canada

Bantam Books are published by Bantam Books, a division of Bantam Doubleday Dell Publishing Group, Inc. Its trademark, consisting of the words ''Bantam Books'' and the portrayal of a rooster, is Registered in U.S. Patent and Trademark Office and in other countries. Marca Registrada. Bantam Books, 1540 Broadway, New York, New York 10036.

PRINTED IN THE UNITED STATES OF AMERICA

OPM 0 9 8 7 6 5 4 3 2 1

For my sons Laif and Eden, with whom I have learned so much.

Acknowledgments

This book could never have been written without the loving support of so many. I especially thank Brian McCusker for his careful daily reading of the pages as they came hot off the word processor. I thank my sons, Laif and Eden, for their frequent cheerful and distracting visits as they passed by my study on their way to and from the surf; and for our other special times together. And I thank my parents for always being there when I needed a break.

I thank my friends, in particular John Reed, who constantly inquired after the project and listened as I shared its ups and downs—mostly "ups" since I found working with these wonderful stories to be an absolute joy.

Special thanks are also due to many others:

David Tai, my acupuncturist and friend, for his loving warmth and exceptional skill.

Therese Reeves for her intelligent transcriptions of the interview tapes, and the conversations we shared while she was doing them.

My agent, Rose Creswell, for her ongoing confidence and advocacy.

Jo Jarrah for her expert editing of the manuscript.

And once again I thank the magnificent team of women at Transworld: Judith Curr (publisher), Marie-Louise Taylor (senior editor) and the very special Maggie Hamilton (head of publicity), a dear friend indeed.

Finally, I warmly thank all the near-death experiencers who have so generously shared their ideas, homes and lives with me over the past five years. Their friendship and support is a continual source of inspiration and pleasure in my life.

Contents

Preface

Three months after the publication of *Reborn in the Light,* Judith Curr, the publisher, asked me to write another book. She wanted me to compile a collection of some of the interviews I had recorded with near-death experiencers (NDErs) over the previous five years. On reflection I thought it was a good idea since I had already received many letters from people who were keen to know more about the experiences of the individuals featured in that first book. Most, of course, had primarily written to tell me of their own near-death experiences (NDEs) or those of people close to them, but they were also intensely curious about the experiences of others.

As I revealed in *Reborn in the Light,* the sort of corroboration that comes from comparing notes with other experiencers is one of the most significant steps to self-acceptance and self-confidence for NDErs. But locating other NDErs or finding alternative ways of getting this validation is often difficult. So many of them have had their stories dismissed as fanciful that they tend to keep a low profile. And it is not only the experience itself that they need to compare—they also need to discuss the following years, which, in some cases, can be quite troubling. The establishment of AUSTRALIANDS,[1] a support group for NDErs, has gone some way toward providing a context within which this can happen, providing as it does the possibility for them to meet with each other. However, for those people who are unable to attend AUSTRALIANDS gatherings, reading the firsthand accounts of other near-death experiencers can be the next best thing.

But comparing stories, noting the similarities, building a better understanding of the phenomenon, is not only an important step for NDErs. It is equally important for their sometimes dismayed families and friends, and for other interested people, whether the source of their interest is personal or professional. I hope that the following collection of twenty stories will further this process of understanding not only for NDErs but for this other group also.

The stories as they appear here are faithful to the accounts of the individual experiencers, although their privacy has again been respected by the use of pseudonyms and the alteration of identifying details. And in each case the transcripts of the original interviews have been edited to eliminate discontinuities and repetition.

The light was wholly enfolding. I was in it and it was in me. It was a sort of oneness of light. . . . It wasn't a subjective feeling—it was a lighting up, right through everything. It was there, it was here, inside, outside, everywhere. And it was total love, enfolding.

It's still with me. . . . When I came to properly, everything somehow seemed too hard, and yet a lot of that luminosity stayed with me. I still felt glowing inside.
—Mary

We are all a part of God, we are immersed in spirit. . . . Each of us is like a cell in the body of God, so we all have God's inherent qualities: love, peace, wisdom, etcetera, but we don't recognize it because we have this sense of separation. But once we can get over the sense of separation we'll know who we really are and then we'll be able to start expressing it. . . .
—Moira

Introduction

What is a near-death experience?

Every individual's near-death experience is unique, yet when a large number of NDE accounts are examined it is found that they tend to follow a discernible pattern. Near-death experiences unfold in stages—the earlier stages being far more common than the latter. As I wrote in *Reborn in the Light*:

The near-death experience is said to occur when a person is close to death (or in many cases actually clinically dead), and yet is resuscitated or somehow survives to recount an intense, profoundly meaningful experience. The near-death episode itself is typically characterized by a feeling of peace, an out-of-body experience, the sensation of traveling very quickly through a dark tunnel, generally toward a light, an encounter with the spirits of deceased relatives or friends or a "being of light," an instantaneous life review, and for some, entrance into a "world of light" (p.3).

Near-death experiencers often report that movement out of the body is the first indication that something has happened. But once out-of-body, there is an immediate sense of peace and well-being. Not only is there no pain or discomfort, but there is often an overwhelming experience of bliss. NDErs describe suddenly finding themselves observing their bodies from a vantage point near the ceiling. Some soon return to their bodies without going any farther. However, among the others, many describe quickly losing interest in the activity around their bodies and seeking the next part of the experience, which is movement through the area of darkness toward a magnificent light.

It is while still traveling toward this light that some experiencers are stopped and turned back by an encounter with the presence of a spiritual being. This most often takes the form of a voice telling them, ‘‘go back,’’ ‘‘it's not your time yet,’’ or some other such message.

Other NDErs may continue their journey through the darkness uninterrupted and actually get to observe, or even enter, the ‘‘world of light.’’ These experiencers describe a beautiful landscape and encounters with deceased relatives and friends, ‘‘luminous beings’’ and occasionally a ‘‘Being of Light.’’ Those who reach this depth of experience are almost always reluctant to return. However, return they do, sometimes very much against their will. But the near-death experience does not end with the regaining of consciousness. Many life changes follow.

In *Reborn in the Light* I have already discussed the many aftereffects described by NDErs. For instance, following their near-death episode, their attitude to death changes markedly. Near-death experiencers have *no* fear of death and they speak of a strong belief in an afterlife firmly based in their own personal experience. Many also tend toward a belief in reincarnation. Experiencers frequently assert that they would never take their own lives, although they express compassion for any who do attempt suicide. And their loss of fear, while beneficial to themselves, often draws them toward working with the grieving, the elderly and the dying.

They describe their experience as spiritual rather than religious and there is a marked shift away from formal religious adherence to private nonformula prayer and meditation. There is a general feeling that they have had personal contact with God or a Higher Power during their experience and that this contact is ongoing in their daily lives.

There is a wide-ranging enhancement of psychic sensitivities following the NDE. For some people this is accepted and indeed welcomed, but for others it is found to be rather overwhelming.

Attitudes to self and others also change. NDErs often describe a strongly developed sense of life purpose. Again and again they say they are sure they have been sent back for a reason. For some that purpose is immediately obvious, but for others, even many years later, it is still not clear, and remains an ongoing source of frustration. Their interests change dramatically. Many want to find out more about themselves, often developing new gifts or talents. And there is a widespread concern with helping others. Indeed, as time passes a more positive view of self generally develops and this seems to overflow quite naturally into changed attitudes to others. NDErs typically appear to be loving, accepting, compassionate and tolerant of others. However, paradoxically it is also reported that many close personal relationships break down under the strain of post-NDE life.

The number of people involved in this sort of transformation is not small. Even ten years ago a survey in the United States revealed that eight million Americans, or five percent of the adult American population, have had such an experience.[1] And, in a prospective hospital survey conducted about the same time, it was found that in circumstances of near-death crisis *more than forty percent* of people report an NDE.[2] In the following stories you will see just how varied the circumstances of near-death crises can be. For instance, both Barbara and Jennifer were young children with pneumonia, looked after by parents at home, when they had their brushes with death; whereas Grace was in a hospital under close medical supervision during a difficult labor; and Shana went into shock because of an allergic reaction during a kidney operation. Michael almost drowned during a surfing mishap and Robert used a shotgun to shoot himself in a suicide attempt. Yet each of these people recognizes themselves as a near-death experiencer, and their stories reveal many similarities. However, there are also differences. Just as there are many paths to any spiritual awakening, there are also many paths to its integration.

Over the past years I have been asked countless questions. Whether following public lectures, during radio phone-in sessions or in the numerous letters I receive, the same questions recur.

"Do children have near-death experiences? What do they see?"

"What happens to people who commit suicide? Do they go to hell?"

"Did anyone have a negative experience?"

"At what point do people come back? Do they want to come back?"

"Do many people get to the other side? What do they see?"

"Are people more religious after their experience?"

"Has anyone had more than one NDE?"

The questions go on and on.

In the following pages, all these questions and many others are answered. The stories are organized into five sections, each focusing on a commonly asked question. But there is no theorizing—the answers are to be found in the stories themselves. The near-death experiencers speak in their own voices, describing the highs and lows—the ongoing awareness of the Light, the moments of clarity, as well as the frustrations and confusions—in their attempts to understand and weave the near-death experience into their daily lives.

CHAPTER 1

Childhood Experiences

I've been to the angels and when I was with the angels there was a mummy angel and a daddy angel, and . . .

Maria was stunned as she overheard her four-year-old daughter comforting a neighbor's child. He was upset because his grandmother had just died.

I saw lots of angels coming and going. I wasn't scared—it was beautiful, with the angels. It's okay, they'll look after your grandma.

Maria remembered well the time two years previously when Penelope had stopped breathing. Although immediately rushed to a hospital, two and a half hours had passed before she was breathing again. She then spent five days in intensive care and twenty-one days in isolation. Although many tests were conducted, it was never discovered exactly what had happened.

• • •

I am often asked, "Do children have near-death experiences?" The short answer is yes. For the *Reborn* study I interviewed ten people who had their experiences during childhood, but at that time, only one of them was still an adolescent. Since then I have spoken to, and received letters from, many others who had their experiences as children. Moreover, during the last year I have been seeking out child experiencers for my next project and have so far had occasion to interview quite a few of them. An encounter with these children is always remarkable. And probably one of the most extraordinary features of their stories is the matter-of-fact way in which they relate them. They certainly remember their NDEs with delight, but they accept them as absolutely normal.

But of course today, much more than in the past, children are able to talk about their experiences and, I should hope, have them more readily accepted. For children in the past this has been particularly difficult. As Barbara said:

I was a little girl who had to be seen and not heard anyway, but to come up with something like that was unthinkable.

When I remarked to Erin, a ten-year-old, how fortunate she was to be able to share her experiences with her parents, she nodded her head sagely, then grinned wryly and said:

Yes, but I think Mum's getting a bit tired of hearing about my Canadian past life.

This of course raises the question of aftereffects. Children, just like adults, have sometimes overwhelming changes happen in their young lives as a result of their experiences. Quite apart from dealing with the problems of physical recovery, they often have the additional challenge of adjusting to, and explaining to others, not only their NDE, but ongoing episodes of clairvoyance, astral travel, precognition and many other phenomena. Many describe feeling different from their peers, with a different understanding of the world and dissimilar values. For parents also, these changes can be quite unsettling. One mother wrote to me:

My daughter, now ten, had a near-death experience when she was five. She told me about it six months later. I was shocked. But considering the changes in her I wasn't surprised. She was very different from the small child I knew before the illness, but I had no idea why.

And Erin's father wrote to me:

For me it has been a humbling experience to have been given the most believable description of life after death from my daughter, a child of nine years of age.

Some people believe that it will be in the stories of children that we find evidence of the near-death experience untainted by cultural conditioning and free of conformity to societal expectations. For this reason there has been much interest among researchers in collecting children's accounts.[1] But, as a consequence of my contact with hundreds of NDErs, I would not expect it to make any difference whether the accounts of childhood experiences are taken from the experiencers while they are still children, or later when they are adults. I have found that NDEs remain genuinely vivid in the memories of experiencers over long periods of time. William Serdahely, a professor of health science, has come to a similar conclusion. In 1991 he made a comparison of children's NDEs and retrospective adult accounts of childhood experiences and found that there was no discernible difference between them.[2]

In the following six stories Barbara and Jennifer describe their early experiences, which, as you will see, are undiminished by the passage of time. Then Michael, who was still a teenager when I first spoke with him, describes his near drowning and its aftereffects; and Gary, Edwina and Denise, who had their experiences during their midteens, relate their stories and describe the changes in perspective that have developed in their lives over the intervening years. In all my interviews I have found the children to be loving, gentle, courageous and compassionate—qualities you will find again and again in the following pages.

Barbara

Shortly after beginning my research I did a couple of rebirthing sessions at an alternative healing center. Chatting afterward with the therapist, I mentioned the work I was doing and asked whether he knew of anyone who had had a near-death experience. He suggested I have a talk with Barbara, the center's receptionist.

We did talk. Again and again. We still meet to talk these five years later. But that first day, when Barbara looked up from her desk and calmly contemplated me with her clear blue eyes, there was a warmth between us immediately. There was a luminous quality about her that impressed me deeply at the time. Only recently have I come across this same quality again—in young children who have had near-death experiences. It made me wonder whether they had all literally brought back some of the Light with them.

Barbara has snowy-white hair and fair skin. She is gentle, softly spoken and obviously a person who feels deeply. She had her experience as a ten-year-old and I interviewed her fifty-two years later.

I had what they termed in those days "double pneumonia." Already I had a long history of lung problems. This particular time—I was at home, not in the hospital—the doctors told my parents they had done everything they could for me, and that I wouldn't last the night.

My first remembrance of the experience itself was that I was floating on the ceiling and I was just so, so happy. The feeling was just complete happiness, complete happiness and overwhelming joy. There really are no words to describe it, there really aren't. And even now, all these years later, I get very overwhelmed at the feeling.

Anyway, I was just experiencing this feeling and my first thought was, "How mean of them not to tell me about this before." I really was a little bit annoyed that they hadn't told me. My thought was, "I would've been here much sooner. How mean!" I was only little.

And then I began to look around. There were two very big old-fashioned wardrobes in the room and I thought, "Oh, gee, Mother doesn't dust the top very well. I can write my name in this, there's lots of dust." And I was enjoying just bouncing around. I had total movement, there were no restrictions at all and I knew in which direction I was going. If anybody had said what shape were you, I would have had to answer that I wasn't any shape. I was just my thinking, knowing, feeling self, in total. And it was just so beautiful, so beautiful.

And then I looked down and I saw this little figure on the bed and I thought, ''Oh, isn't she little? Aren't I little? That's me.'' And that was okay, that was fine. There was just acknowledgment that that was me down there, but I *knew* I was really in total ''up here.'' But then I thought, ''Now I'm going to do something and I can hardly wait. I'm going, I'm going!'' And I was just absolutely thrilled. I was bursting with anticipation and joy that I was going now. It was like going home.

I say today that I made one mistake. Today I wonder what would have happened had I not looked back, because what I saw when I looked back was my mother's face. My father was sitting on the left side of the bed and my mother was on the right side, and it was a long, long way down. As soon as I looked at my mother's face, I knew I couldn't do that to her. And as soon as I decided that, I was overcome with a wave of disappointment. I was just *so* disappointed, beyond words. And then there was nothing. I must have been back in my body because everything stopped. Everything stopped. I feel deeply moved even today just thinking about this.

That experience was real, absolutely real. I knew I was very sick, I knew that that little girl down there was very, very white and I knew I had already left her—I knew I was dying. Initially I felt total joy, bliss and a perfection that I can't put into words, but then there was this overwhelming disappointment at having to return. I remember it very clearly. It's just as clear now as it was then.

I didn't want to go back to my body, absolutely not. It was like being let out of a cage for the first time. Remembering, even now, how I felt when I realized I had to go back, is painful. There was no way I *wanted* to go back. And when I found myself conscious again, I felt heavy, I must have been very sick. I can't relate the feeling I had out-of-body to anything else I've ever felt.

I never ever spoke about it to anyone, especially in those times. I was a little girl who had to be seen and not heard anyway, but to come up with something like that was just unthinkable. So, I must have shelved it, it seemed to go out of my memory. But it came very much to the fore in the last seven years and I would share it with my daughters and they were fascinated by it. Sharing it was a very special thing and my eldest daughter, Loraine, especially was very open to it. Now I know why it came back at that time. Three years ago Loraine died.

Looking back to when I began remembering it again, it's like a picture was shown to me: "Okay, you had that when you were ten, you didn't talk about it, you didn't want to talk about it, you put it in the back of your mind and you forgot it for a while and now in the next few years Loraine will die, so here it is for you to look back on, you need it." Now I look back and I see that's why it was presented to me. That's why I could share it with her and my other daughter, and that's why it was enjoyed so much. To have had that experience, to have had that knowing and that loving was a wonderful comfort to me, absolutely. So much so that I wonder how I would have coped without it.

Before my experience I had never heard of such a thing. I had a very confined life—my father was an atheist and we were not allowed to go to Sunday school or anything like that. I had absolutely no idea. I think as a child I thought, "Oh, this is life, and it goes on forever." I didn't fear death because I never thought about it. I didn't question it at all. But now, consciously, I have no fear of death, none at all. To me, death is not to be feared, nothing to be feared. In fact I think it's something to be really anticipated because I believe that this is not the only life I've had and it's not going to be the last one either. I've read a few books on reincarnation and it seems to me to be the only thing that fits. It seems to me to be the only answer.

When she was quite young Loraine once said to me, "Mum, would you like to go first or last?"

I said, "Where?"

She said, "Would you like to die first or last?"

And I said, "What a question! Your life's ahead of you and I've had mine. Certainly you will go last."

She just gave me this look I'll never forget—it was just a sort of half smile. And she said, "Mum, I wouldn't like to be last."

Now I have a great interest in learning more about death and dying. When Loraine died I felt I didn't know anything much about it. I was with her for twelve months before she died, virtually day and night. In the hospital they let me sleep on the floor and be with her. But I wasn't aware of a lot of things that I'm aware of now, so that my deepest regret is not being able to help her die with ease and grace. Now I'm very interested in learning about that. I have visions of going this year to spend some time with Elisabeth Kübler-Ross in West Virginia. And I would like somehow to work with the dying.

I've always thought of the experience more as spiritual rather than religious. I had no religious training with my parents, but my situation was unusual. My sister was born twelve months after me, and when she was born I think my parents asked somebody to look after me, and I was with those people for five years. They wanted to adopt me. Those years are the only years I can look back on with wonderful, happy memories. During those years I was taught to say my prayers, grace at the table and there were lots of religious books. That was the only religious training I had and it was something I looked forward to and loved and accepted. And when I was returned to my parents it was like going from the sublime to the ridiculous. There was no grace. The word *God* was not mentioned in the house. It was a very difficult time for me. So I did in fact have a spiritual start in life, but then that was suppressed.

Today I describe myself as spiritual, not religious. I meditate a bit, but I don't attend church, although I suppose if I've got a form to fill in I still just put Church of England without thinking.

Before my experience I'd never heard about psychic experiences, but I did feel I was in touch with another world as a child. On those occasions I felt different, I felt really alive. Some evenings I played with fairies in the garden. My aunty would sort of get down with me and we'd just go around together. I could see the fairies. That was very real to me, very real.

Now I definitely believe psychic experiences occur. I've had other out-of-body experiences but only during rebirthing sessions. And I had a rebirthing session once in which I could hear music, incredible music, which I knew was the language of the soul. It was the only music in the universe, the only language in the universe, and I remember laughing to think that we, on this plane, called our "language" a language. It was so funny.

I also know how people are feeling when they walk into a room. I am very aware of the energy that people bring in—I pick that up very quickly. Now I pride myself that my intuition is pretty accurate. And that's increased. When I was a girl I was critical, I seemed to be very critical and judgmental. But now I can meet somebody and really look at them and really appreciate their beauty and see them. I've changed a lot.

I often have the sense of being looked after, and at those times I say to myself, "There you go again, you worried for nothing.'' And I reprimand myself. I'm continuously, consciously aware that I am not alone.

Since remembering that experience and especially since Loraine's death, it's like one day I was going in one direction, that happened, and then I changed direction. It's been like an opening of myself.

I used to worry about what other people thought of me—it was absolute torture. Now I don't. I used to worry about material things, but now that's not so important. It's good to have a job, but it's not as important as it was. I was a single parent and I brought up the girls, just the three of us. So given that set of circumstances, I'd had to be very careful, watch the money, go to work, and it wasn't easy. But I've relaxed on that a lot, certainly in the last few years. Now I know that what I need will be there.

When I was a little girl, after my NDE, I felt I was different from my peers and it was very hard to make friends—especially in school. I felt so isolated in school. Oh, it was an uncomfortable feeling. I didn't like being different, but I was and I knew I was. And I always felt with my family that my family was there and I was over here. Always. I suppose that was because of coming back from where I'd been. I never felt part of the family. I never had many friends and I could not relate easily to many people, but nowadays I find that I've changed, that I can relate to others, with empathy. And it is sort of confirmed in my job, because people come in just to talk to me.

Since remembering the experience, I've read a lot. I did a course in acupuncture, I did a rebirthing course, I did the Elisabeth Kübler-Ross seminars, things I never would have thought of doing before.

As a child I felt like I was in a little black box, but now my life is good. I live alone in a small flat, but I have a wonderful job and that's very fulfilling. I see my daughter and her children occasionally—they've recently moved from the city and that's beautiful. There's something, though, that is not clear for me. At the moment I seem to be marking time. A few years ago I was taking big strides, big strides and suddenly I've stopped and sometimes I could scream with frustration. Sometimes I could scream out, "*Why?* Show me what to do!" But I know it's only me and I know it's got to come from me. At the same time I think, "Gosh, I've only got x number of years now and I really need to use them." I really do need to use them. It's like, *"Show me, will you!"* I feel very frustrated because of that.

I feel great admiration for anybody who can actually do something. The two areas that I feel drawn to now are, one, working with dying people, and if I'm guided to dying children then that would be just so right. I really feel for children. Whether I'll be working for children from here on, I don't know. If I did find work with children that would be wonderful, because that draws me. And recently I toyed with the idea of going to spend some time in countries where assistance is needed, particularly with children.

I think of myself as being very blessed to have had that experience, very blessed to be able to take it and keep it in my mind all the time, which I do. And if there's a way I can use it—and I just know there is—I know that that's what I'm going to do in the future. When I get out of this vacuum, I know that this experience I've had will help me. I just know it. I think of it as being one of the most significant experiences in my life.

I feel now that I didn't die when I was a child because if I'd died, I wouldn't have had my children and I wouldn't have been here to be with my daughter when she died. And I also know that there's something that I need to accomplish before I go.

• • •

Two years ago, after a long spell in America nursing a dying friend, Barbara began working as a volunteer in a large city hospice. She feels there is still something more she will be led to do.

JENNIFER

I was returning from a long trip during which I had driven about two thousand miles and interviewed many near-death experiencers. This was to be the final interview before returning home. I drove into the small coastal town where Jennifer lives—it was so peaceful I could hardly bear the thought of moving on the next day. A wide river flows to the sea, there are miles of bushland and beaches, and close behind this coastal strip is a magnificent escarpment. Set between the escarpment and the beaches are several streets of small, neat houses, and these are divided into two sections by the river—the larger township and more affluent houses on one side, and the quieter, simpler "fishing village" environment on the other. Jennifer lives on the quiet side.

When I think of Jennifer I think of her amiability, her kindness and sweetness of expression. She greeted me affectionately, as though we had long been friends, and sat me down in her living room among the packing cases—she was preparing to move to a house a couple of streets away. Her daughter and grandson were also present and we chatted for a while over a cup of tea before beginning the interview.

Jennifer was seven years old at the time of her experience and I spoke with her forty-six years later.

At the time, being so little, I didn't know that I was so sick. I had pneumonia, very seriously, and I found out later that I was so ill the doctors left me there in my bed to die. They didn't even put me in the hospital. They just left me there and told my mother I was dying, that it was just a matter of time. When she asked if there was anything she could do, they just told her she could give me eggnogs with brandy if she liked, but they didn't think it would do any good. All I knew was that I was tired and I just wanted to sleep all the time. I only remember regaining consciousness once, and there was my mother trying to give me a drink.

I had what seemed to be a dream in which I saw this lovely white stairway with a lot of blue around it, kind of misty, cloudy. And I saw this lovely lady coming down the stairs in a long, white robe, and she had a beautiful face and I recognized her instantly. It makes me go goose bumps just to think of it even now. Anyhow, she said, "Don't be afraid, Jennifer."

And I said, "I'm not afraid, Great-grandmother."

She said, "You know me?"

I said, "Yes, Great-grandmother."

And she said, "Take my hand, I've come to show you the way." And she stretched out her hand to me.

I said, "Oh, I'd love to come with you, Great-grandmother, but I can't go now, because Mum needs me and she's got no one to look after her but me." I said, "I can't come now, but you come for me later when Mum doesn't need me anymore and I'll go with you then."

Suddenly it just all disappeared and she disappeared and I woke up and saw my mother standing on the veranda outside. We lived in the one room high up on the second floor of a building. And I saw her, she seemed to be going up and down, like a ship in the sea, and I thought it was an earthquake. I screamed to her, "Mum, come off the veranda, it's an earthquake!" She came running in—she thought I was dying.

The tears were running down my cheeks. I was so upset that I had to refuse my great-grandmother, not go with her. And she said, "What are you crying for, Jennifer? Everything's all right. Don't cry.'' And I said, ''Oh, it's just because I had to say no to Great-grandmother. She asked me to go with her and I told her I couldn't go, I had to look after you.'' At that Mum started to cry like anything. I said, ''Don't cry, Mum, I'm all right now, I'm all right.''

While it was all happening I wasn't the little girl in the bed anymore. I couldn't distinguish how I got to be with Great-grandmother, but I just knew I wasn't in the bed anymore. I knew I was up there, somewhere with her, standing. I so wanted to go with her, she was so lovely and I knew I'd be safe and happy forever. Mum and I had had some tough times, and I knew that if I went with Great-grandmother, there'd be no more tough times—I'd be happy and there'd be no more sadness in my life, ever. So that's why I cried when I woke up. I knew that I could have left all troubles and fears behind, but I chose to stay with my mother.

I was all right after that, and the doctors couldn't understand how I recovered. But I knew. I said to Mum, ''I know why I recovered—it's because I asked Great-grandmother not to take me, and she didn't. So I'm all right.'' And it was quite clear to me. But the funny thing about it is, I'd never known my great-grandmother. When I was being brought into the house as a baby, she was being taken out on a stretcher because she was dying. They stopped the stretcher so she could cuddle me in her arms and hold me—I was the only great-grandchild she ever saw. But naturally I never saw her, I didn't know her. During the experience she had a younger face than I would have imagined my great-grandmother to have. I have now seen photos of her as a young person, very young, and I've got some of her as an old person, but I never actually knew her.

I believe Great-grandmother had been sent to get me. I think she must have somehow requested to take this little child that was part of her own family so I wouldn't be afraid. And when I requested to stay, I believe that she was allowed to leave me here and not take me.

I believe there was a purpose for me living. So much would've been different if I'd died. I never would have become a writer and I know I've made a big difference to my husband's life. And then there was someone else who loved me very much in his life and I was the only love he ever had. He died, but I know my surviving meant a lot to him in the short life he had. And my daughter wouldn't have existed—she's brought such joy to her young man—and my little grandson. There's so much! I can look around and see the difference it would have made to so many lives if I'd gone.

I can't be sure of what my life's work is, but I do believe there's a purpose for me going on and I believe I won't go until that purpose is fulfilled. I believe I have to stay alive to fulfill the things that I've got to do. I don't know what they are, I just go on the way my life seems to go, carried along with the tide (laughs).

I've told a few people about it. My husband is a bit ESP-ish, and my daughter, too, so they're very understanding about these things. Actually I've never been ridiculed about it by anybody—I've even spoken to strangers, other writers, about it. I've never seen much written about it apart from bits in magazines and things like that, but I have found those interesting—finding out what happened to other people. But I still haven't read a lot.

Before the experience I'd never thought much about death. As a child it never worried me because my mother taught me that prayer "Now I lay me down to sleep," and that covers you for death (laughs). So I only knew about death because it was in my prayer, but I always thought that if I did die, I'd be safe, I'd be all right. It never worried me at that stage, because I hadn't had a lot of people dropping dead around me or anything like that.

Now I believe that at death our souls join up with those we've loved in this life. Because of my experience I believe that there is another life. It won't be as we know it. Although we won't have the substance of our bodies, we'll still see people in a spirit way, just as if they were as solid as us here. I know this because I saw Great-grandmother as solid as you, and since then I've seen this other young man I loved. I've seen him like in a dream situation and I've heard his voice as clear as anything. He died of cancer, but when I see him he's young and well again, and fit. I don't fear death now at all.

As a child I went to Sunday school. I wasn't sent—I wanted to go myself. When I was little my mother bought me a book called *Jesus of Nazareth.* It wasn't a Bible or anything, but it started me asking questions. I'd hear the family talk about church—they weren't going at the time—and suddenly one day I said to my mother, "I think I'll go to Sunday school." So I just did, and from there on in Mum said if I wanted to, I could. That was Methodist, my grandmother's religion. My mother's religion was Church of England, but I thought that might have been a bit heavy, a bit close to the Roman Catholic. I worked that out for myself. I was much more advanced in my thinking than my age would indicate—I seemed to be an old mind in a young body.

Now, funnily enough, I *am* Roman Catholic (laughs). I married into the faith. I didn't have to become one, but I thought, "I don't like divisions in the family with religion. Oh, blow it, I'll be converted." So I was (laughs). But I don't go to Mass, I've got my own beliefs. I like to have a mind of my own on things, and explore. There's a lot of mixed-up things that have gone into church religion. It's not all factual, a lot of it is fairy stories. I don't think we should be led by religion.

I'm sure my beliefs were affected by my experience. They would have to be because from there on in I really wasn't afraid of death. I always knew that someone there loved me.

I have had many psychic experiences since the NDE, although none before. At one time when I was very ill, that young man I've talked about used to come to me in the morning, just before I'd wake up, and tell me things. Once he said, "You're going to have to fight for the right to live." And this was before I knew I was so ill and that I *would* have to fight for the right to live. I've been through some very hairy times and experiences, and I did have to fight. He also told me there were things I still had to do. So I quite believe that those I have loved have come back to guide me. It's happened many times. I have sort of a sixth sense about things, and I get warned of dangers. I believe one day I won't be warned of something or I won't be told. I mean, I'm not immortal, am I?

I've had several warnings of dangerous situations. Once I had this warning—it's just a feeling that goes through me that I can't do a certain thing—while I was swimming at Brighton-le-Sands. I swam there a lot and I was never afraid of sharks. This particular day I went out of the water, and I couldn't make myself go back in again, and I called my husband out. He asked what was the matter and I told him I felt there was something wrong. I said, "I can't go back in that water." He's always trusted me in these things since I told him about something else that happened earlier in my life, so he said, "That does it—I'm not going back in either." When we got back up to my mother in the car, she said, "I'm glad you came out because I saw something dark in the water near you.'' The next day, we got the Sunday papers and on the front—I'm getting goose bumps again just thinking about it—the headlines were splashed: SHARK AT BRIGHTON-LE-SANDS. Apparently the alarm bells had gone off and all the people had to get out of the water. Yet at the time I hadn't seen anything, it was just a strong feeling.

And then another time, there was that earlier experience. I used to work as an usherette and I also worked in shows in town, like amateur theatricals, and I'd come and go up and down this street in Ashfield every night. All the time I was traveling at night, and I'd walk up and down the streets, and come from the trains by myself in the dark, and I was never afraid. This night I'd just gotten near my home, and there was a little lane I had to go past—I was never afraid going past this lane—and it had a door on it (someone had the funny idea to stick a door across this lane). I was never afraid, but this night I could *not* go past the door on that lane, I had to cross right over the road. Anyhow, the following night, an elderly lady from our boardinghouse was walking past that lane, and a fellow jumped out, bashed her up and stole her handbag. And she died, from the bashing. I thoroughly believe that he was there the night I felt I had to cross the road. I've thought about why she should be killed and why I should survive, and I feel that it must have been her time to go, and it wasn't mine, and that's the only reason I was safe from it. Of course I did take notice of the warning, but that was the very first warning I'd had like that, and I thought that if I told other people about it, they'd think I was mad, or that I was just scared. But when that happened to her I felt awful that I hadn't said anything about it except to my mother. But I couldn't know that that would happen to her.

Ever since my NDE, all through my life, I've sensed things, dangers and things like that. I believe if there's something going to happen and I'm meant to get the warning, I'll get it. If I'm not, I'll get clobbered (laughs) and fate'll catch up with me. It just happens, I don't go looking for it. It comes to me.

I've also had two experiences of flying. Once I was flying around the top of the lounge room, near the ceiling, and I was looking down, and I thought, "Wooh . . . that's lovely." I liked that. And then another time, much earlier, when I was a young girl, long before I'd ever been flying anywhere in my life, I dreamed I was flying without any airplane or anything like that. It was just me, flying over land and green grass and roads and things. It was lovely, I adored it. I thought it must have been a dream, but it was so real, it was lovely, a lovely feeling of freedom to be able to fly. Now I go flying all the time, in aircraft, and those two experiences are the only "seeming to fly by myself" experiences I've ever had. They were more real than a dream, they were terribly vivid.

One thing I do have that annoys me terribly is that for ages now I seem to be talking to strangers every night in my dreams, or listening to strangers talking. And it annoys me really because I don't know them from a crow, and they yab, yab, yabber away in my dreams, and I'm getting all their conversations and I wish they'd just all go away. They're having very earnest conversations and I don't really want to be in them at all. When I wake up I don't know for the life of me what they've said. I don't feel as though I've had a restful night, my dreams all cluttered with these strangers (laughs).

I'm really enjoying life today. I still don't know my life purpose, but I have things I'd like to do and achieve. I would like to entertain people with my work. I'd like people to be able to read it and enjoy it. It would be nice to have enough money to help the family so we'd be comfortable, because we've been battlers, but material things are not important. I don't want wealth for wealth's sake. I don't want to be a millionaire. I just like to be comfortable, that's all. Just so we've got enough for our needs, so we don't have to worry about where the next meal is coming from—which we've had [to] a lot.

I make a very sparse living out of my writing. I get a lot of publication, but mostly they want it for free or for very little, and it's only recently the prizes have picked up to anything worthwhile. I've won lots of prizes, but I didn't get much money out of them.

I started to write when my daughter was about seven, but it was very rough. I had some good ideas and occasionally sent off a storyline for television, and they used them. It was encouraging to see that my work was that good, but I gave TV away and concentrated on ordinary books and that kind of thing. I'm in anthologies with other people, but my work is very scattered, with anthologies, newspapers, magazines, competitions. I've only got one book out on my own and that's in the National Library. I won a radio short-story competition, and my daughter won second prize! We stopped counting after seventy-two awards for her photography and art, so we might not be rich but we're never bored.

I think I'm such a lucky person, to have such a lovely family, and I love my writing. I like to help other writers. I like to give them a hand in any way I can. One of my other great interests is aircraft. I do volunteer work with the "historical flight." It's entertainment enough for me—I'm the only woman who works on restoring vintage aircraft. I get there and get the rust out of the old aircraft. I've always been interested in flying, but never did any when I was younger—I couldn't afford to do it. But now . . . I like my lifestyle, it's exactly the way I would like it to be, except for the money worries.

• • •

I think the most important thing to come out of my near-death experience was the strengthening of my beliefs in something beyond this world. I *know* that the ones I've loved will all be there to welcome me when I go. I *know* we don't just exist here, and that's all.

MICHAEL

I had just given a talk about near-death experiences at a meeting of the Theosophical Society. I had already spent some time answering audience questions but, once that was over, found myself surrounded by a group of people who wanted to talk to me personally—either to ask more questions or share their own experiences. Among this group of mostly middle-aged people I was intrigued to see a quiet young man waiting on the periphery. I was concerned that he might leave before I was able to speak with him, but he seemed to be interested in what the others were saying, and he stayed. When finally we spoke, he revealed that he'd had an NDE during a surfing mishap four years previously, but that he'd never yet told anyone about it.

A few weeks later I went to talk with Michael at his parents' house, where he lived. We sat in a sunroom at the back of the house surrounded by orchids. Michael is of medium height, fair, with long, blond hair. There is a stillness about him and a gentleness of manner that struck me as unusual. It was soon clear that his quiet demeanor had its source in centeredness rather than diffidence. He spoke openly of his experience and its life-changing aftereffects.

Michael was fifteen at the time of his experience and I spoke with him four years later.

I was out surfing by myself. I have to admit there was a pretty big surf. I was out on one of the surf-club malibus—big long boards—and I was just mucking around. There was a really savage shore dump. I went down a wave, nose-dived, and went sailing off underwater and got pinned on the bottom. I was sort of pinned down on my back, and I couldn't move. And there was no leg rope, so the board couldn't drag me away. Then I started swirling around, caught up in the whitewash. I seemed to be really getting into trouble and started losing my breath and panicking. I was thrashing for the surface, feeling my lungs going in and out, trying to breathe. All of a sudden it just stopped. I can't explain it—it just stopped. And I thought, "Ah!" And I opened my eyes and it was all white.

I thought, "Ah, I'm dead." And I felt really happy. I was floating around. And then, I don't know if I closed my eyes or whether I blacked out, but everything went really dark and I felt really peaceful. I felt great, as though the worries of the world were lifted off my shoulders. I can't explain it but it was all dark, and I felt as if I knew what I had to do. I didn't see the light but I could feel it, if you know what I mean. I couldn't actually see a light but I *knew* it was there and I knew what I had to do.

And then I started seeing again, and I was seeing where I was from above the surf! I couldn't actually see my body, I just knew it was down there. But when I was looking it was different—usually when we look with our eyes we see one thing, but I could see everything, the whole beach. I was looking around and I sort of got this feeling, it's hard to explain, as though I was a part of it all. I felt as though I was a part of everything around me. I just felt as if a bit of everything was in me and I was in everything. I remember feeling sorry for the people walking along the beach, because they didn't understand. I felt it was really sad that they didn't know this sort of thing happened. And that's when I went down. I didn't actually want to go down, I was more or less dragged down.

All of a sudden I was dragged back into my body again. I didn't feel the sort of panic that I left with. I still felt very peaceful inside. Even though my body was going hell-for-leather, I was still very calm inside. I hit the surface gasping for air. I'd been under the water apparently for about two and a half minutes. I shouldn't have come back up after that time. When I came up I felt just horrible—I wanted to go back. Eventually I got to the beach and lay down for a while. I felt sorry to be back.

There were people on the beach who saw me. They weren't lifesavers, they were just normal people watching, but apparently when I was down for so long they were getting worried.

I haven't spoken about the experience with anybody. I think I've been afraid that people wouldn't accept it. And anyway, I think it's a very personal thing. It's not something you could go around telling people.

Before the experience I didn't really think about death much at all. I was pretty young. Death isn't really something to worry about when you're young. I think I took death with a pinch of salt, like most kids. But now that I know what's going to happen, I'm not looking forward to it exactly, but I won't be sorry when it comes. And I'm not afraid of it at all. The only fear I have is of the pain before I go. You know, the brief period like when I was panicking. That was pretty horrible.

I think there's a reason I didn't die. I honestly don't know what it is yet, but I think it has something to do with that feeling sorry for people, because that's what actually took me back down to my body. It's possible it has something to do with that.

• • •

I think of that experience as a spiritual one, not religious. When I was a kid Mum used to stick us in Sunday school, Church of England, but I wasn't religious at all (laughs). Even now I'm more spiritual. I disagree with the church. I went for a while, because one of my friends is a Christian. I went with him for a while, but some of the sermons I disagreed with completely. They were wrong as far as I was concerned, so I left it.

I express my spirituality in different ways. I go bush-walking a lot by myself, because I tend to get the same feeling as when I was above the surf—I feel sort of at one with everything. I can get the same feeling in the bush by myself. I just sit there—it's only very brief, but it's worth it. And I do a martial art which is an esoteric martial art. The training builds willpower and strength, but the esoteric side is very good. They don't actually teach us anything specific, they just encourage us to go out and find what we believe in and work with it. Find out what we believe is right and go with that, rather than filling our heads with ideas. My parents think I'm mad because nothing really bothers me. Failing exams and that sort of thing. Nothing really eats at me.

I've had many psychic experiences since my NDE. I've had some amazing ones, but normally just a lot of little things happen, like sometimes I'll jump before I hear a loud bang. I've done it at work heaps. There'll be a really loud bang and I'll finish my jump before it actually happens (laughs). People sort of look at you and go, "Ooh!" Sometimes I just know things are going to happen and they do—important things and little things. Like with my tech electives, I remember one year I did three electives and I dropped two. And I remember thinking, "I'll do the other two next year." Yet every time I thought of the next year, I kept thinking of doing three electives. Then I'd think to myself, "What am I on about? I've only got two to do next year." I ended up missing the exam, so I did have three to do the next year after all. Just little things like that happen all the time.

One of the strangest experiences I've ever had happened one night when I just couldn't get to sleep. I was rolling over and over. I was sort of trying to get to sleep, and all of a sudden I got a feeling of pressure in my head, my eyes just clenched really tightly, then it just went blank, totally black. Next thing I was looking through a little hole, and I don't know where I was or what I was doing, or what I was looking at. I can't really describe it now, but it reminded me of a leather-bound book. I don't know whether it was a book or a pile of papers, but that's what I got the feeling of. I went down, really close to the leather, and then I went into it. And then I was going down into each page, and while I was in each page I could look at it. I knew everything that was on the page as I was going down page by page, through the whole book. I was going actually into the paper and I could see everything on each page, and there was writing there that was "illogical." I don't know if you've seen drawings of steps going everywhere, and things that aren't supposed to work out, but the writing was like that. I still can't even work it out now. I remember looking at it, saying, "Oh wow, it's amazing!" And there were sort of blueprint drawings, and really funny drawings that I couldn't make out. And then, I don't know why I did it but I suddenly thought, "Oh shit!" (laughs), and then I went *bang,* straight back. I can remember every little bit of it. I wasn't asleep, I know that for sure. It was incredible.

I've had out-of-body experiences a couple of times, too—once in my sleep, and once in meditation. I've learned to do a meditation where I imagine I have a glass body—the outside's glass and I fill it full of mist. And then I slowly bring the mist up into my head and then concentrate on it. I found it was hard for my head to actually take that. When I first did it my eye muscles went into spasm. I don't know why, maybe they couldn't take all that energy in one place. I was told that after a while, doing this meditation, I'd find that little things would happen.

Anyway, this night, I was lying down in bed meditating, and all of a sudden I felt something happening in my head. I looked and there was a hole in my head, and I thought, "Oh yeah, let's see what happens." And I pushed all the mist out, and that's when all the muscles in my head sort of crunched up. That was really noticeable, like my eyes just closed right up, and my whole head was shaking, and I pushed it all out. And then I imagined myself in the training hall. And then I was just there. I had a look around, the place was empty and the lights were out. Looking around, I knew it really was the place because I could feel it, it's just got an amazing feeling, it's really strong. I knew I was there, so I had a look around, and then I just came back.

And one other time in my sleep, I woke up and found I was in the hallway, floating around near the ceiling. I went down the hallway, looked around the lounge room, and looked around the kitchen and then just went back to my body.

I'm quite good at helping people, too. I haven't had much experience of healing other people's wounds or anything, but I'm very good at helping people, talking to them if they've got problems. I'm very good at that. I seem to know the right thing to say at the right time. I don't think much about it, but I sort of feel guided when I'm doing that.

In my life generally I definitely feel guided. That's why I don't bother about anything. My mum sees it. She's got this feeling that I've just sort of off-loaded everything onto something else, or someone else. I suppose I've got the same feeling. I just don't worry about anything. I know everything will turn out right, and I usually know what's going to happen anyway.

I feel I'm being guided all the time, but especially if I'm in the bush. There I feel I can communicate on a feeling level. It's sort of hard to explain, but I know I'm being taught, I'm being taught with feelings. And now I can feel what's going on for people, too. Not all the time, but a lot of the time I can feel them. Now if I sit down and talk to my brother, I'll sort of feel what's going on for him, and put the same feelings on myself, and it makes an empathy. There's definitely a great sense of empathy.

My attitudes have really changed since my experience. I used to have to wear the right clothes, puff out my chest for the girls, all that sort of thing. But I don't now. Vanity's gone out the window completely. I don't care anymore, I don't dress up or anything. I have a pretty laid-back attitude. I just sort of think that where I am now and what I'm doing now is just a passing moment of time, so impressing someone else doesn't really matter, because tomorrow it's not relevant.

I feel much more confident these days and my interests have changed a lot. In the surf club there are still lots of girls hanging round, and while before I used to puff out my chest and ask them out—everything was about having a good time—now I don't bother doing it anymore. One of my main interests now is horticulture (laughs). I had no idea what I was going to do when I left school, but after that experience I signed straight up for horticulture. I'd never thought about it, I had no idea what horticulture was! I also joined the Theosophical Society. I got sick of church and then one day I saw a talk advertised in the Theosophical Society's bookshop and went along. I got into it from there. My friends think I'm really off the planet.

I also used to be in the Wilderness Society—that's a branch of the peace movement. I'm not for violence but I'm not actively seeking peace. I understand that the violence is a part of where we live, it's a part of this world, it's something we have to come to grips with, that we have to accept. I tend to think it's another vehicle for learning. Yet violence to the environment still affects me. The logging of wilderness areas is an emotional issue for me. I feel strongly because I know how much is left, and doing horticulture I know how fragile it is.

I think since that experience the most prominent change for me is being able to feel, and to believe in my feelings, which I never did before.

Gary

I first met Gary on a cool spring evening at a huge Victorian bayside house that he shared with a number of friends. We had already spoken by telephone to make the arrangements, so he greeted me in a friendly manner and then we went straight to his room, where, soon after, we began the interview. Gary is quite small, fine-boned and elfin in appearance. His thick, fair hair falls over one side of his face, and he seems to be filled with a strong nervous energy.

Gary had his experience as a sixteen-year-old and I spoke with him sixteen years later.

There were quite a few things going on that year. I'd gotten to a sort of crossroad in my life in general, mainly because the interests I had were incompatible with the interests in my family background. My mother didn't want me to go to a general high school, mainly because there were girls there (laughs), and she didn't like this particular high school anyway. She felt that because my two brothers had gone to a technical high school, I should go there as well. But my interests were a lot different—I was interested in paleontology, geology and things like that, while my oldest brother was mainly interested in electronic things and my middle brother was only interested in drinking and chasing girls. But I was quite serious-minded. At that stage I was in Year 10 and I just felt that everything was going the wrong way. I don't know how it came about, but things seemed to get out of control, with my general unhappiness and my inability to socialize. I actually kept to myself quite a bit. I was right on the edge all the time. Even in the group I hung around with, they thought that I was quite strange. The problem was, I didn't know what to do about it. Then, in the end, I got quite ill and I almost died.

There is a family history of diabetes on both sides, and my diabetes came on over a period of about six months. I started getting thirsty and urinating a lot, and then that went on until it became quite bad. One particular morning I just had to go home from school. The day before that was the first time I couldn't survive forty minutes without needing to ask to go to the toilet. What would usually happen was that I would just hold on for that forty minutes for dear life—I couldn't even concentrate on the schoolwork. But I didn't want to ask to go to the toilet because by that time my friends were cottoning on to the fact that there was something wrong with me. They were making fun of my constant need to go to the toilet and so I was a bit sensitive about it. I'd just hold on. In the end, four or five times during the day I'd had to get up to go to the toilet during the period. I went home that night feeling miserable.

The next morning I got up, went to school, but I was so ill that I had to go home again. The doctor came and visited a few times, but I just got worse and worse and lost lots of weight. I had actually gone down from 145 pounds to 89 pounds or thereabouts, in the space of that six months. I'd been interested in weight lifting, but I got weaker and weaker until I couldn't lift the weights that I normally could. I just thought everything was going wrong and I didn't know what to make of it. But then, during the week after I went home—I didn't go back to school at all after that—I got weaker and weaker and worried quite a bit about it. The doctor would come around and say, "There's nothing really wrong with you, you've got a bad cold, a bad infection." Of course by that time I *did* have a bad infection because I'd started to get pneumonia, I was so weak.

One morning, the doctor looked me over and said, "You've just got a bad infection and you have to have a penicillin shot. Take some of these vitamins and you should be all right within a week." And I said to him, "Well, don't bother, because I know I'm dying, and you're not telling me." I thought by then that I had cancer or something, and he wasn't telling me. He just stared at me as though it really frightened him. I could tell from his eyes that he was really frightened by what I said. And he said, "Well, I'll give you the shot. Give me a ring if anything goes wrong." He gave me a shot and he went.

Sometime after that—I don't think it was very long, maybe an hour or so—I was lying there and suddenly my whole life flashed before my eyes. It basically seemed like everything appeared there for an instant and my whole life was being reviewed, just like that. It was most puzzling in the sense that I didn't know what to make of it. I just remember the utter amazement I felt. But now, looking back, I think of it as the least significant of the experiences, in terms of how it affected me emotionally.

At that stage I didn't say anything to my mother. I actually couldn't communicate very well at all because I was starting to go a bit delirious. I was probably starting to go into the coma. I don't remember actually going into the coma or anything, but between that time and ending up in the hospital in intensive care was when these other experiences happened. Basically, there were three other experiences. They were really quite powerful and they affected me quite a bit. In the first one I found I was out in front and above a big building, and then I was above the ambulance and above myself being taken in, and then that faded out. The next thing I was inside the building that later on turned out to be the hospital and I was floating down the corridor. This was late at night and I think that that must have been the first day. After that there were a lot of experiences of going down a tunnel with light at the end, interspersed with experiences of being above my body, traveling along the corridors and being above the hospital—not just in the room but right above, outside. In actual fact when I came out of the coma and went down to the ward that I was in for the next two weeks, I traveled along the exact same corridors—I knew that I'd been there before.

And then there was another experience where I was actually above my body and that was the most vivid one of being above my body because then I recognized very clearly that it was me down there. And the nurse came over and said, "Gary, you have to drink some orange juice." One minute I was up there and the next minute I was right in my head, because she was starting to force it into me. She must have just pulled me right back into my body and I just went, "Aargh!" and everything seemed to be closing in. I'd been really pulled back in, looking back on it quite fast, and it was quite painful.

As well as those experiences there was another experience that I find very hard to conceptualize. I seemed to be in a state of, I suppose you could say, luminous presence or something like that. I suppose it's almost like, the sun hasn't quite come up, and you're just staring out to sea, and the sun's not actually in the sky and it's just daybreak, it's like a clear blue sky, whatever, but in the experience it wasn't blue or anything. There wasn't any conceptual process going on while I was experiencing this, there wasn't any reference point, no I, no me. There wasn't even any thought process, no mental events going on at all. The other thing was that I had an intense feeling of well-being, which for me created a really strong impression because I'd never felt that, I'd never had that feeling. Since, though, sometimes in meditation I've touched upon it, but then I've messed it up by grasping at it too strongly. There is an intense craving to get back to that feeling. Other things, even sexual experience or anything like that, just take second place. The experience of luminosity was extraordinary.

When I came out of it I just wanted more, but at the same time I didn't want to say anything to anyone because I thought I'd automatically be labeled crazy, or they'd think that I'd had some weird experience. Even though I didn't have any more experiences after I came out of the coma, I'd lie in bed at night and go through the visual imagery, wondering whether I should say anything, or whether I was going crazy. So I didn't say anything to anyone, not to anyone.

After I got out of the hospital I actually went around to different churches, I even went to a Jewish synagogue. I really sort of investigated various religions, the Bible, whatever. I tried to sort out what the whole meaning of life was. It had become very important at that stage. I'd almost died, and therefore I realized life was really precious. But what did it all mean? Then one day I went into Woolworth's and there was a book sale going on. I picked up this one book, *The Teachings of the Compassionate Buddha,* and the first words I ever read of Buddhism were in that book. Basically it said, "All you are is a result of what you have thought, it's founded on thoughts, it's made up of your thoughts." And that just hit me like a ten-ton brick! I'm not joking, it just hit me like a bomb. And I just thought, "This is amazing, this is it!" And there I was, only sixteen, and never heard of Buddhism in my life.

I thought, "This really means something, me picking this up." So I went to my mother and said, "Look I want to buy this book, it's only fifty-nine cents." And she said, "You don't want that, that's absolute garbage!" She'd been a Sunday-school teacher, but for various reasons her religious interest had been knocked out of her, she'd virtually given it up.

We used to go to Sunday school until about the age of six, but then stopped going. But I never had much of a religious background, and never had much of a feeling for God or anything like that. But there I was with that book. I came to the conclusion at that stage that everything came from myself, all the experience that I had. And then, of course, when I opened the second part, I came across this particular part called *The Thousand,* and there it says, "Even though a man may overcome the 1,000 x 1,000 men in battle, he who overcomes himself is the greater warrior." At that moment I just realized what a complete mess my thoughts were, and that really pulled me into line. And I thought then, "Well, it's all up to me!" Even though that felt like a relief, it was also very hard, trying to grapple with all those things. It really made me feel quite disturbed for a while.

Last year I got pneumonia again. I make spinal braces at a children's hospital, and I really had a lot of work on. It can become quite an intense situation because a child's spinal deformity can move at an incredible rate and they'll often need a brace within, say, four weeks. I got quite weakened by the stress. Because of my weakened state, the memory of that experience just started coming back. Of course it didn't come back with the power that it had at the time, but I thought about it quite a lot. I had become really depressed with the pneumonia and had begun to doubt all the things that I was doing in my life—whether I was going in the right direction or whatever. Just having the memory of that experience really provided the impetus to keep going on my spiritual journey. I realized that life is short.

Even at a very early age I remember being aware of the fact that life is short, and that you die. Between the ages of five and seven I would lie in bed at night and I'd just think, "I'm going to die any moment." I'd just lie in bed and think of that, and then in the end I used to dread going to bed at night because I'd have to face up to these sorts of thoughts. For two years I was really quite disturbed by them, and yet I didn't say anything to anyone. Then at the age of sixteen, death was suddenly the big thing again, but after that experience there was no fear, no fear at all, even though I was still trying to grapple with what had happened.

Today I have a fear of dying, but I don't have a fear of death. I suppose what I'm saying is, I have a fear of pain. But that experience of luminosity has a stronger pull—that's obviously what I want to rediscover. It reminds me that I should keep going on my spiritual path. In actual fact I've made the decision to leave work next year. I'd like to go to India for a while, and to study Tibetan Buddhism. It's strange because over eleven years ago I took this job thinking I would soon leave to go to India, but circumstances developed in a strange way and I became quite good at spinal bracing and got all these ideas for taking measurements and X rays, and of course I became really involved in what I was doing. Suddenly one day I realized that my original intention had fallen by the wayside. But now I've decided to go.

I believe now that what happens after death is what I experienced. As far as my experiential understanding goes, that's all there is. The rest of my beliefs is just a collection of intellectual bits and pieces I've put together since. The feeling during that time was actually just a state of pure and total presence. I was just completely present. I was just there, and that was all that mattered. Looking back, I remember the feeling of well-being that

I had during the luminous experience. Afterward, sometimes I had moments when I actually doubted that I'd experienced it at all, experienced any of it. But now during meditation and just in my everyday life, that luminosity experience has really become quite important. I develop quite a bit of power just in the memory of it.

As far as why I didn't die is concerned, I am of two minds about reasons, in the sense that I believe that things can happen to people that are out of their control, and things can happen to people that are within their control, and both of them seem to be inextricably interwoven. Where one point meets the other, I don't know. I don't know whether that experience had a purpose other than what I would give to it. I suppose I feel that the experience is the result of lots of circumstances come to fruition, call it karma if you like. However, once I had that experience, I did feel that it meant a lot. But whether it came about because there was a divine plan or a plan via some sort of luminescent being or supersoul or whatever, I don't know.

The experience was significant in that it showed me there's a different dimension to the mind that we normally don't take any notice of. It opened my mind quite a lot because at that stage I felt completely cold toward everything—I perceived there was a total lack of love in my life. The experience really catapulted me into something quite different.

I didn't tell anyone about it until five years later. I am very different from the rest of my family in terms of the way I think, so I couldn't tell them. But when I was twenty-one I went to a Buddhist community and it was there it occurred to me that I *could* talk about it in that setting. In actual fact I was surprised how accepting of it they were, even though they hadn't had experiences like that themselves.

• • •

Over the years I've become quite intuitive. Since that experience I've found that I have an ability to tell what people are thinking. A lot of my patients' parents tell me that they find my intuition about their family situation quite extraordinary. In my job I rely quite a lot on that rather than relying on great medical theories. I believe that love and affection and compassion and generosity really heal people. So that's the way I act toward the children who are my patients.

When I was a child myself, I was always quite distant from everyone else, and quite closed in—for a while they even thought I might have been autistic or something like that. And I had to wear a leg iron until I was ten years old. So I suppose my sensitivity about myself and other people became a primary concern from an early age. Now whenever I see other people suffering, it always affects me deeply.

I've been told by one psychic person that my hands emit quite a bit of power. In my job I work a lot with my hands, making and fitting spinal braces, so in some ways my hands have real significance. When I'm fitting the brace, I actually spend quite a lot of time in close proximity with the child, who is seminaked the whole time. So I have to build up trust. Most of the time the contact only comes from bending them over or moving them around to see how flexible their spine is. But in fact while they're standing there I talk to them and rub their back. I feel it's important, it seems to be a natural thing to do. Most of those children need that type of thing, they need some sort of sympathetic touch, not just sympathetic words, because touch is more powerful. I don't think about it much, it just seems to be something that needs to be done at a certain time, so I do it. I feel the most important thing is to get them to accept what's happening to them—that they've got a problem, that they have to wear a spinal brace but that they can still get better.

• • •

I'm still not sure how the experience connects with my ordinary everyday life, although I've begun to realize over the last two years that it's important to keep it alive in my life rather than just to let it float off somewhere. I think the greatest change for me has been finding my spiritual path through that experience of luminosity. But I'm sure it's not only meant to be of benefit to me. It's for others, too.

EDWINA

My first meeting with Edwina happened on a cold, rainy night outside the rooms where she lived in a big inner-city house. She had just arrived home with a friend at the moment I approached the front door. Despite the weather she smiled broadly, said hello, then erupted in laughter at her efforts to open the door while juggling her umbrella and bag. She talked constantly as we entered her place, dumped everything just inside the door, then proceeded to clear a path for us through an accumulation of books, papers and other odds and ends. She then stopped, raised both hands in the air in an "I give up!" sort of gesture, laughed heartily, excused the mess and made us a cup of tea. Her exuberance and good humor filled the small room. All three of us finally sat down on the floor around a low table to do the interview.

Edwina is a law graduate working in the field of corporate law. She is of medium height, with short, light brown hair, bright clear eyes and a broad grin. Her first near-death experience, which she barely remembered, occurred when, as a three-year-old, she contracted typhoid fever. She experienced her second NDE when she was fifteen, during an operation for cancer of the thy-

roid. We spoke ten years later, when she was twenty-five.

I had a major experience when I was fifteen. When it happened it was like a remembrance of what had happened before.

I was coming out of the operating room—it happened in the recovery room—and I just remember going. I sort of floated off from myself. I found I was looking down at myself, and then I was flashing to a place that was all light, like nothing but hundreds of colors and lights—but not like that—that's the only way I can describe it. It was like going through a tunnel, like shooting through something and seeing the light at the end. I heard a sort of whooshing sound, like fast wind or something like that—a sort of *whshshshsh.* It was like every wind and every sea combined in a torrent, but not deafening, not like a deafening roar. It was sort of like silvery moonbeams and the noise they'd make on water if they were going to make a noise. You know what I mean? A sort of brushing sound.

At the end of the tunnel I saw floating patches of light. It was like all of those patches of light were entities of some kind, but they were all part of one thing. I suppose they were like amoeba or something, all attached together but still with some sort of definition (laughs).

Then I remember being in the light, just suddenly being totally engulfed by the light. I'm saying "engulfed," but it was very nice. I could perhaps say "subsumed"—I'm trying to find positive words and use them in the right sort of way. And suddenly I had the feeling that everything was okay, everything was perfectly all right. That was the feeling I remember most. I had the sense that no other feeling in the world was worth that feeling. I can say it's the most beautiful thing I've felt in my life, but in saying that, it's just words.

The feeling is not just a process of thoughts, it's not intellectual. That's the difficulty I'm having, like when I put it into an intellectual frame of mind, when I try to write it out on a bit of paper, I'd say well, it wasn't actually this head that was thinking it. It was something different, totally devoid of intellectualization, totally devoid of the little boxes that we put things into. I suppose it's like trying to describe an overwhelming passion. But it's not a striving sort of thing. It's not a striving passion, it's like a passion that's just there. It was wonderful.

The next moment I was coming back, and then I was suddenly back in my body, fighting off this oxygen mask, which apparently had failed to work (laughs). I think I was *made* to come back. I don't think I really had any choice because I didn't have any intention of coming back, but somehow or other I ended up back here anyway (laughs). For years it stayed with me that I didn't really want to be back. I don't feel as intensely about it now as I did, but I think when I was seventeen or eighteen, it was very much a case of "I don't want to be here!" (laughs).

It's so difficult to describe. I feel that my whole being, my soul energy, my very essence, was touched upon in that state. It seemed to bring about an opening of my psyche and understanding of the world. And that feeling has stayed with me, it doesn't go away. Sometimes suddenly I flow back into it, it gives me so much energy that I feel I have the perseverance to go through anything, at any time. And now, especially when I meditate, I have the feeling of total communion, a oneness with every piece of energy in the universe, whether it be negative or positive. It almost gave me a sort of amoral attitude to life. I now have the feeling that there isn't any separate good or evil, but there is a combination of opposites, and that everything is necessary.

I didn't talk about it much with others, it didn't seem necessary. I talked about it with my grandmother—she came out to Australia soon after my operation—but she had a deep understanding of that sort of stuff anyway, so it was easy. But most of the time it wasn't necessary—it was like a little secret that I just kept to myself and let flower. Trying to tell anyone about it seemed to be something that would take away from it, or destroy it. It was too precious. I still haven't read anything about it (laughs). It seems that everyone who hasn't had one wants to read about it! But I always think if I compare [mine] with other people's experiences, it might detract from my own.

Of course at the time, I knew I could die. I had cancer, so I'd gone through the whole thing of having a terrible fear of dying, and knowing I could die, whether it was in a week's time or in two days' time, or whenever. I didn't know whether I was going to have five years or the rest of my life, that sort of thing. Being young, I dealt with it as though it was a sort of dream. Finding out that I had to have an operation, and going through the whole thing, was dreamlike. But when I had that experience I didn't think I died, I just thought, "This is great!" (laughs).

I've felt ever since that what I am inside and *who* I am is very different and divorced from the physical body. Although people usually identify themselves with their body, I don't. In fact I tend to float out of mine quite a lot still.

My ideas about death have obviously changed. When I was very young I was always interested in death and dying. I had a maudlin fascination with death as a child, absolutely maudlin. I used to hang around in graveyards. Members of my family still tease me about it because from the time I was about three till I was about eleven, I used to spend hours looking at old gravestones. You know, total fascination, totally morbid. My mother used to sort of cope with it and take me off to graveyards. I really was totally, morbidly fascinated with it all. But by the time of the experience, that had changed. I'd been brought up High Church of England—I grew up with the fear of God but I wasn't particularly religious. I don't think I had any belief in heaven and I thought death was like a big black wall—no continuity between past and future—it was the end.

But now I think, "Well, when it happens it happens and that's fine." I don't want it to happen too soon though, because now I feel I have things I really want to do here. I don't want to have to come back! (laughs). I'd rather like to get everything all tied up here, and then go. But I'm quite happy about it. I think if it's going to be like the experience I already had, then I'm going to have a jolly time (laughs). I believe now, at the very least, it's just a resting place, a long resting place, and all this thought and panic we put into our lives won't matter anymore.

I have no fear of death at all, but I would never commit suicide, because for some reason I think that if I committed suicide, I wouldn't end up in that place, for some reason I wouldn't end up where the light was. I might end up sitting in the tunnel waiting to go back (laughs). It's just a feeling. But anyway I've got too many lovely things in this life to look after and work on, to think of doing such a thing.

Now I consider myself to be a very spiritual person—it's more important to me than anything else. Last year I was involved with a spiritualist church, mainly because there were so many other people there who were experienced clairvoyants. I found a sort of communion there. I'd been having a lot of difficulty dealing with what was going on in my head, so it was great to be with people who were willing to accept anything, however strange. But not anymore. Now I have a very strong view that church and religion are totally divorced from spirituality. It doesn't matter what sort of religion. They can't help individuals along the path to understanding. The only way that people can find that understanding is by looking within themselves, and looking further within and further still. Most religions I feel take people away from that. I do believe in Christ, though, and I believe in God, but not in a traditional church God. I believe that all that light is what we call God, and Christ is a symbol of the ability of humankind to elevate themselves to that state of light.

Nowadays I meditate and I do healing, clairvoyant psychic healing. And I pray, but now I pray to an internal, rather than an external, god. However, I am still very open to other spiritual paths. I might find they're not for me, but I still want to understand them and learn more about other spiritualities.

Before the NDE I really identified strongly with my mind—I was always very highly developed intellectually. Now I try to find a balance between spirit, mind and body, but the balance at the moment is very much biased toward the spiritual. This has been very much the case in the last couple of years. So I suppose the body is still lagging slightly behind (laughs). I've always had a very low self-esteem in the physical world, and I sort of still do. Working in the corporate law environment, all the male partners think if you're not tall, thin and blond, you're not worth talking to. I get upset about it occasionally, but then I think, "Hang on, that sort of thing's not important." Apart from that I'm usually really positive about what I've got to offer. But I realize it can't be offered to everybody and it's not something that everyone understands.

I have a strong understanding that the experience gave me certain gifts—very, very, very important gifts that I can help other people with. I'm sure that the calm and peace that comes with that sort of understanding can be spread around and used to help teach other people in different ways. It took me long enough to realize it, but now I know I need to have my whole life built around that understanding. That's why I'm giving up work. After the NDE, when I'd finished school, I took a year off. I'd been so nurtured and so controlled by my father that I had my whole legal career mapped out for me. I just sort of slipped back into achieving, but from then on I couldn't take it all so seriously. You see, material success is not important to me. If I wanted material success, I wouldn't be giving up law. I could earn hundreds of thousands of dollars a year in the sort of scene I'm in, but I know it would kill me. As you can tell, I'm not really into possessions, more into a lot of old junk (laughs), but not material possessions.

I know I've been given a very intellectual mind for a reason, too, so I'm not trying to deny that. But now that I know this legal work isn't right for me, it's all a matter of trusting that the right thing will appear in time. I know it'll eventually become incredibly clear, but I still need more time. I haven't decided yet what I should do. I don't know whether I should go off and do courses in natural medicine and stuff, but a lot of things people learn about in those courses are things that seem already to be second nature to me. They just happen and I just understand them without learning about them. The experience has given me a huge wealth of knowledge. The hardest thing for me has been not knowing how to use it in the world.

I always knew psychic things could happen, mostly because of my grandmother, who taught me to read hands when I was about four years old. As a child I always knew that I could see things. I used to see places before I went to them, and then when I got there I'd know that it was the place I'd dreamed about. That sort of thing used to happen a lot, but not to the degree it does now. Now it happens all the time. It's increased even in the last year.

I have a couple of friends who I communicate with telepathically. It also sometimes happens with people I don't know very well, but I usually try to be very careful about that sort of thing. It's too dangerous to open myself up to everybody, but with my special friends it's really nice. I think my intuitive sense was in slumber for five years, while I was sorting myself out, but in the last two years it's been particularly strong.

I've had many out-of-body experiences since my NDE. Sometimes when I'm really very in tune, I can actually push myself out to go and visit people, not just by telepathy, but actually be there. But I don't do that often. I only do that when it's very important, when I'm in trouble or something like that. On the other hand, sometimes I'll have an out-of-body experience when I don't expect it. It usually happens when there's a particular group of people that I know very well around me. Then I feel safe, I know I'll be called back, and won't get lost out there somewhere. It happens, or I do it, probably about once a month.

I do trance mediumship but not very often, only once in a blue moon these days, purely because you have to have the right people around you and do it for the right reason. I did some on Sunday night but only because it was for the right reason at the right time. The same thing applies to the healing—I only do it when it's needed. It mixes in very much with the trance channeling because often the healing is part of that. It's seeing things and explaining things to people. It's knowing where people's pain and anguish are coming from at a deep level. It's being able to explain it to them, and get rid of it by making them aware of it, and then pushing it out. But it has to be with someone who is vulnerable to that sort of energy. It can't be done with someone who doesn't want to change. I seem to be told when to do it and the right way to do it, and of course everyone needs something different.

All of this makes life the best thing in the world. It makes me feel that life is worth living. I feel I really have something positive and beautiful to offer. I don't know how to explain it, but I have compassion for everything and everyone and it's like overwhelming love, but not love that needs. It's *unconditional* love. Understanding unconditional love is one of the greatest things. That would be the most lovely thing that I could teach anybody. If I could give them even one second of the feeling of unconditional love, that's what I would like to do. Sometimes in healing I can get them to that point where suddenly they experience that one second of unconditional love and that one second can often be enough to make them want to go back and find out how to get there themselves.

These days, if anything ever gets to me or starts worrying me, I like to be amongst trees. Feeling their energy is enough. I've only just moved to the inner city recently, and it really got me down to start with. But now I've found a little park to go to down on the point, and then of course there's the harbor and the zoo. I go there almost every weekend and I find that's great. I don't like seeing animals in pens, but I do love the animals and being amongst the trees. I love it, I couldn't appreciate it more. In fact, except for work, my lifestyle is bloody good! (laughs).

What I like best is spending quality time with the people I care about. From my near-death experience I learned that love is the most important feeling in the universe. Love, love, love. I mean, that's what had the most impact on me as a person. Love is the most important thing in the universe, and sometimes that feeling is so strong it makes me cry, sometimes it makes me laugh. But whichever way you look at it, it's just fantastic!

Denise

Denise had traveled from Queensland to attend a conference in Sydney and we'd arranged to meet at her hotel. She is tall and imposing, with short, blond hair and rather aquiline features. Her eyes in particular are noticeable—they are pale blue and very piercing. One has the impression that she is able to see straight through anyone or anything. We talked for a few minutes in the lobby, then went up to her room to do the interview.

At one point during the interview her husband returned to the room. She asked him to go out again to do something, explaining after he left that she had never told him about her near-death experience: "I thought he'd just take it as foolish nonsense."

Denise has always maintained contact since our interview. We have exchanged many letters and phone calls, and have even met again on a couple of occasions when one of us was traveling interstate. The day after our interview, she ended up in the hospital after having an allergic reaction to medication she was taking. Although there was a period of unconsciousness, she did not recollect an NDE on that occasion. However, as she later said, "When I regained consciousness, decisions had been made." She knew she had to leave her violent marriage and make a new beginning. She also knew that everything would work out.

Two months ago Denise was married again, this time to a fellow near-death experiencer, and a few weeks later we all met again at a gathering of NDErs.

Denise was seventeen years old when she had her

experience and we recorded the following interview twenty-four years later.

I was involved in an automobile accident. My girlfriend and I had gone away for the weekend and we were on our way home. I'd been driving for about five hours when she asked me if I'd like her to drive. Unfortunately I said yes. I didn't think to ask her if she had a driver's license since I didn't think you'd make an offer like that without one. She'd only taken the wheel for a matter of moments when she got into the gravel on the left and overcorrected, cut across to the right and rolled the car, which then continued rolling down a bank. In the process I was semi–knocked out, but I was coming and going—I wasn't completely unconscious, I was sort of halfway. The driver was bruised but not severely injured, whereas I had spinal injuries and I'd put my foot through the window, ending up with major lacerations and the almost complete severance of one toe. While the car was rolling I also knocked my head many times, because in those days seat belts weren't compulsory.

We were fortunate that a truck driver happened to be coming up the hill toward us, saw the car rolling and had a radio to call the ambulance. And again we were fortunate that an ambulance had actually been delivering someone home to that area (about an hour's drive from the city). So the ambulance was soon there. At the time I was wafting in and out of consciousness.

So I was admitted to the hospital and taken to the operating room, where a young doctor and nurse began to suture my foot. I sort of felt like I was leaving my body and looking down on them. I knew that was me down below, but I also knew the important part of me was up where I was. I hadn't had any anesthetic or anything, and I was really quite concerned because I knew they were going to operate on my foot to sew my toe back on. I was trying to say to them, "Listen, I really am quite conscious, you know, this is going to hurt. I really don't want you to start sewing me without giving me something to kill the pain.'' But they were obviously not communicating with me, they were flirting with one another. (After I came back I made a facetious comment to the doctor about this. He went white with shock and was speechless. He appeared embarrassed, but didn't discuss it further.)

Anyway I was sort of looking down at them, but I just wasn't reaching them. I can remember then—I really don't know how to describe it—I was sort of first of all looking down over what was happening, but then it became an *Alice in Wonderland* type of experience, looking down a tunnel. I felt a black, spinning, falling sensation, but then it changed to a rising sensation. There was a momentum being gathered. It was very dark but not at all terrifying, and I was being pulled upward through a tunnel that became brighter and brighter. There was this light at the end of the tunnel. It was yellow/white, more white than gold, but indescribable and beautiful. It was a person, but not a person; a god, perhaps, but with no real shape. I took the person to be God, but God of all, not just one religion. It was a really pleasurable experience. I was conscious of someone speaking to me but not with words. It was a thought-transference type of arrangement. I was met at the thoroughfare, and wasn't allowed to go past, and I was told, ''No, you're too young, you have a life of service in front of you. You must go back.'' I felt a deep sense of regret at that, but I knew I couldn't argue. Normally I'd argue with people, but this was a final sort of decision. It wasn't something that you intervened in. I didn't want to let it go, but the choice wasn't there. I felt very rejected at first. I wanted to hold on to the experience, but it seemed I wasn't up to scratch, you know. I felt I was being told, ''You go away.'' I felt great disappointment and a profound sense of loss. But later, when I recovered, I became curious and began to wonder what was meant by "a life of service," because at that stage I hadn't really done much.

In the meantime I had been taken away from the operating room. I had died. My parents were notified that I was dead and my father was severely shocked—he had a heart attack. My aunt, who knew the ambulance driver, was coming in to visit, to see how I was getting along. She didn't know at that stage that I was dead. But it was she and my uncle who finally came in and found me. I was just lying there naked on one of those stainless-steel trolleys, in the morgue. By then they had been told I was dead and presumably they had come in to identify me, but when they put their heads around the door I looked up at them! I had never been so cold, and I asked them for a blanket.

It just seemed a peculiar sort of experience, but very pleasurable. It seemed to be a process of transition. At the moment when I felt the deep sense of despair and rejection, I was quite aware that I was at a crossroads, I was quite aware that that was the point where one died. But there wasn't any fear, and since having that experience, death has no fear associated with it. I have been working with dying patients in my job and I know I can share my experience with them. They sense that death doesn't hold any fear for me and therefore they feel able to talk about their own death. I think usually people are just afraid of the unknown.

I was a child at the time it happened and unaware of anything similar, so I was quite embarrassed about it and thought I must have been losing my mind. I just couldn't understand it. Even though I felt it was a very significant experience, I didn't discuss it with anyone. I didn't want anyone to belittle it. It was to me a pleasurable, moving and very intense experience.

Later, when I began working in psychiatry, I thought

maybe it was some sort of enzyme reaction or some chemical imbalance related to shock or stress. I didn't tell anyone about it till twelve years later, when I read this thing in the *Reader's Digest* at work. I was just so stunned that I said to the people in the room, "Oh, but that's just what happened to me!" It was sort of an involuntary reaction. We started talking about it, but I still didn't say a lot. After that I didn't discuss it with anyone again till I mentioned it to my supervisor during my training for the postgraduate diploma in counseling.

Even now I don't really like to talk about it. It's just that to me it's a personal thing, like for instance an orgasm, that you don't go telling everyone about. It's pleasurable, but it's personal. It wasn't that I was ashamed of it, it's just that it's always been something very private. I'm not even really interested in reading about it. I read something in the newspaper recently and it was just so stupid that I thought, "Well, as far as I'm concerned, this is my experience, I know how I feel, and it's totally irrelevant to me what other people think."

Before I had my near-death experience, I hadn't really thought about death much at all. I suppose I just had the usual community attitude that death was final, and very black. But then, after that, I changed my view completely. Now I know that death is not a frightening experience.

At one time a few years ago, I became quite depressed—I just didn't know where I was going, but I wouldn't say I was suicidal. I see a lot of suicides in my work. I think sometimes death is okay, whether it's a natural death, such as throat cancer, or assisted death, as in suicide. I just will not take the stance that people must be made to live at all costs. But I could never take my own life, because for me that's a given. When the time is right I know it will be taken, whether it's tomorrow or in twenty years' time. So for me, suicide was not an option, even though I believe it's quite an okay option for anyone else. I suppose that sounds very odd.

I was brought up High Church Anglican, so there was a lot of hellfire-and-damnation stuff. After the NDE I rejected that. I just felt that previously, to me, God was a very alien God, and after [the NDE] that just didn't hold water anymore. To me it was almost as if the slate was wiped clean at that point of arrival, and everything started afresh after that. To me God is no longer a judgmental being. After [the NDE] there was an anger and rejecting of religion, and I've never really gone back to it. I don't attend church. It's almost as though I feel I've got the answers. I know that sounds very superior—it's not meant to come over that way. It's just that when some ministers stand up there and preach their sermon, I can't accept that now. So that's why I separate religion and spirituality. I feel that some people just haven't got it right.

I have a lot of psychic experiences. I was very, very close to my father, and I always knew how he was going—we could sort of communicate without communicating. And sometimes I'll get up to answer the phone and it hasn't rung, and I'll say, "Oh, I'd better answer the . . . ," and before I finish the sentence the phone starts to ring. People find that really quite odd. Sometimes I'll be quite wrong about who's calling, but I'd say about eighty percent of the time I'll know who's there. Other than that, though, I usually only have experiences with people I'm close to.

Once, I remember, in the early seventies, I woke up in the middle of the night and said to my husband, "Oh, there's this terrible fire!" and I described everything that was happening, and the people that couldn't get out. He said, "Don't be stupid, you're having a nightmare." And then in the morning we heard on the news that there'd been this dreadful fire in Belgium, and everything I described had happened. I really can't understand why that occurred except that I did have a Belgian pen pal. I never heard from her again, so I presumed that she died in that fire. It was a terrible sort of feeling, it was almost as if I'd been there—I could smell it.

I have an amazing sense of being looked after. But I also have the attitude now that when something's bad, it's only a temporary thing and I'll grow from it. I've had some terrible experiences in my life—for instance, I was sexually abused as a child and again raped as an adult—but I feel that these experiences have helped me to help others. I work a lot with people who have sexual problems, and I feel that some of the experiences I've lived through have helped me to be a better counselor. I am more compassionate and much more understanding of people who are in difficult circumstances.

I feel now I am living a life of service, very much so. It's not deliberate, it's just like that. These things seem to just happen, but underneath it all I always feel that my life is directed. And I also feel an obligation that "as you take from life, you must return."

I'd always wanted to work in psychiatry, because my uncle died in a psychiatric hospital. There was this feeling of helplessness and not being able to connect that drew me toward psychiatry, much to the shock and horror of my family. So by the time I had the car accident I'd already done three semesters of occupational therapy, but the NDE then gave me a reason for it. Most of my interests are now involved in helping others. But sometimes I feel I need to have periods of time out, and this is something my husband doesn't understand. I love to have people around—that's not the issue—but sometimes I like to withdraw, just sort of be on my own. A lot of people can't understand that privacy doesn't necessarily equal rejection.

My lifestyle today is really hectic (laughs), yet in

some ways I'm more settled within myself. I think going back to study as an adult gave me a chance to reassess where I was at. In 1983 I started studying again. I started to think about where I wanted to go—I suppose it was a middle-aged sort of thing. That year I decided to do an MBA, but I also wanted to do counseling, so I enrolled for both, thinking that whichever one I was selected for would be the right one. But I was selected for both, so I still couldn't make a decision. I was going to drop out of one of them, but I didn't. There certainly wasn't any spare time, but I realize now that it was important to do them both.

I have very strong views on many social issues. I feel that everybody has an obligation to contribute what they can to life, to mankind. But obviously some people are unable to contribute, so others need to balance it out. This applies even in our own lives. I know that in one part of my life I took, and now I give. I feel people have a responsibility to look after themselves wherever possible, but I also feel the government has a duty to provide welfare for those that need it.

I think abortion is okay, but given the proper circumstances, obviously I think contraception's better. You see I really hate to see abused children as a consequence of an unwanted pregnancy. I think euthanasia and suicide are okay, too, so to me, quality of life is what is important, not just the maintenance of life no matter what.

I suppose the most significant changes to come about for me since my experience have been in my attitude to death and being spiritual. And of course now I do understand what is meant by a life of service.

C H A P T E R 2

Suicides

Suicide is an emotion-laden word, and as a cause of death it inevitably conjures up an image of great distress and despair. Early NDE researchers seemed uncertain of what they would find in cases of attempted suicide. For instance, Raymond Moody, in 1975, reported that he had encountered "a few cases" and that their "experiences were uniformly characterised as being unpleasant".[1] However, in a later work, he found that the issue was much more complex than he originally suggested.[2] And in terms of content, Kenneth Ring, on the basis of eight cases, initially found that suicide-related near-death experiences tended to fade out before the transcendent elements of the experience were able to unfold. But after closer consideration, he suggested that since most of these suicides were carried out with the assistance of drugs or drugs and alcohol, it might well have been their drug-related nature that led to them being aborted, or that interfered with their recall.[3] He finally concluded, however, that there was no relationship at all between how a person nearly died and their NDE. That is, whatever the cause of near-death crisis—suicide, illness, childbirth or car accident—once the NDE begins to unfold it always follows essentially the same pattern.[4]

Near-death experiencers have always been adamant that they would never take their own lives, and suicide attempters in particular have often expressed gratitude that they were not successful in their attempts to kill themselves. This attitude has been found to stem not so much from relief in having escaped a fiery fate, but rather from the understanding that any problems they were hoping to escape in premature death were not going to disappear. As Kate[5] said:

I don't feel judgmental toward people who commit suicide, but I do think if you commit suicide you're leaving something that's not finished and you only have to come back and go through it again.

I have often been asked whether suicide attempters have near-death experiences, and if so, whether they are hell-like. It seems that in our society there is an expectation that people who commit suicide will be severely punished in the afterlife. Despite the many complicated issues associated with the taking of one's own life, this punitive stigmatizing attitude seems to be the one that comes to the forefront when a suicide occurs. Needless to say it is the source of much anguish for family and friends left behind.

Recently I appeared on a radio talk show during which near-death experiencers were asked to call in with their stories. A call was received from a woman who very hesitantly began by apologizing that she had not personally had a near-death experience but still wanted to speak with me. She went on to relate that her son had committed suicide six months earlier and she wanted to know whether I had spoken with anyone who had had their experience as a result of a suicide attempt.

Fortunately I was able to share with her the positive stories told to me by the three suicide attempters I interviewed during the *Reborn* study. However, I was also careful to point out the lesson learned by these suicide attempters (and other NDErs), which was that suicide was not and never could be the answer to their problems. Not one of them believed that they would ever attempt suicide again, although they expressed great compassion for anyone who did, and felt sure that other suicide attempters would be welcomed with love just as they were.[6] After all, as so many NDErs have reported, we are not met at death by judgment and punishment, but rather, by the Light—the source of love, *unconditional* love, forgiveness and wisdom. As one of Raymond Moody's respondents said:

A lot of people I know are going to be surprised when they find out that the Lord is not interested in theology. . . . He wanted to know what was in my heart, not my head.[7]

This chapter will reveal the stories of three suicide attempters—Bill, Virginia and Robert. It will describe the background of their suicide attempts, the details of their near-death experiences and their aftereffects. It will be seen that, rather than being punished for their individual acts of attempted suicide, these three people all had typically positive NDEs that provided each of them with a unique opportunity for spiritual awakening, and led to a profound transformation of their lives.

BILL

I first heard about Bill through a mutual friend who told me of his experience one day while we were talking about my research. The next week I visited him to conduct the interview.

Today Bill is radiant, golden. He is over six feet tall, with fair, curly hair cut short. His skin is a honey-gold color, smooth with the warm sheen of robust good health. He has rosy cheeks and soft blue eyes. He is of solid build, and looks younger than his forty-something years. He is friendly, quick to chuckle and has a look of gentle naïveté that I am sure contributes to his youthfulness. He welcomed me to his beachside flat and we sat on the floor on cushions to talk—for hours, with an occasional break for herbal tea and, as I remember, an especially tasty papaya. He was pleased to be able to talk about his experience with me and, on several occasions since, has been willing to share his experience publicly through newspaper interviews and film projects. "If it can help someone I'm happy to do it," he would say.

Bill was thirty-two at the time of his near-death experience and I first met him ten years later. He now recognizes that his suicide attempt was a result of his active alcoholism, but at the time he was unable to see beyond his depression.

In a blackout I went into a state of depression. I couldn't relate to anything or anyone at the time. I isolated [myself] in a rooming house in the inner city. I think I'd been there for a few days, just locked up in my own head, not going anywhere. The relationship that I'd been in was fast deteriorating, and I didn't know what tools to use at the time to get myself out of the mess I was in because of my alcoholism. So I isolated [myself] and I thought, "Well, I'll stay put." It's all I could come up with at the time.

This day the people who lived next door came looking for me, saying, "Let's all go down to the hotel." I thought, "Oh no, I don't even want to do that anymore." That shows how low I was. At the time I'd been getting pills and different medications for my nervous system. (I realize now that this "nervous condition" was related to my alcoholism and drug addiction.)

I heard them knocking on my door and I wouldn't answer it. They finally got the landlord to open up and I was just sitting there on the bed with my head in my hands, in deep depression. "Come on, let's go out, let's go out." It was something I really didn't want to do. But I had no control, so I finally went along with the party, eventually to a hotel in the backstreets.

I suddenly found I had this buildup of resentment. It just started running amok in my head—jealousy and other insanities. I think on that particular day I was drinking scotch, not the beer or bourbon and Cokes I usually drank. I don't know how many I polished off, but at that stage of my life it wasn't really giving the effect that I'd been used to. I very rarely took my pills out of the house, but that day I had them with me.

There was an argument at the bar, and I had an argument with Pauline (my friend at the time) and I just walked. I didn't say anything at the time. I walked from the bar and went into the bathroom, and I remember looking into the mirror and seeing all the despair and the madness. I just took the whole bottle of Serepax, straight down, a brand-new bottle, which I think was quite a few tablets of thirty milligrams. Mixed with scotch it's pretty lethal—I felt sure the tablets would do the job.

I went back to the bar and sat on a stool. And all I remember after that was that one minute I was there, then—it's like a flash in my mind now—I was outside lying in the gutter. Then I remember the sirens. I don't remember being put into the ambulance, but I do remember them trying to make me walk from the ambulance. Suddenly I had all this unbelievable energy. I suppose you could say it was like putting a pin into a balloon, just letting it all out. All I remember was that five or six white-clothed people had hold of me and they needed a lot of strength to hold me. I don't know where all of this energy had come from. But then, at the same time as the energy came out, it also sapped, and that's when I got carried in and ended up in a hospital room.

I remember at one stage floating near the ceiling above my own body, for quite a while actually. I wasn't disturbed about it. I felt very light, very light. Oh yes, it was excellent (laughs). I felt lighter than I've felt in my whole life.

I just thought, "How amazing, there's me down there." And they've got this contraption, they're giving me electric shocks, and they're jumping on me and using a stomach pump.

At that stage I went back into another, a different zone, where I was lying down flat. I'd sort of come from the ceiling, not back to my body, but back to another dimension where I was lying flat on my back. And if you can imagine it, where I was it was like a trough, like a flat piece of wood that could go on for eternity. Well, I was in the middle of that trough. I was lying on my back, and I could see through the back of my skull, it opened up like a vision. Unbelievable! Just thinking back, it's quite incredible. It's like different prisms were being used to focus out the other way. So as I looked through that way, I was traveling along this trough and I wasn't frightened. I felt, actually I felt a lot of peace, I felt a lot of relief. I didn't think about anything really. I was just in the hands of whatever.

Not being fearful or scared or worried about the experience, I traveled slowly toward what I still describe to this day as a large diamond. And I pictured myself as an ant, small in comparison to it. Only I wasn't just looking up at it like an insect—I was getting closer to it and I just couldn't believe the beauty of it and the radiance of the beam coming from it. And I thought, "Wow, this is incredible!" At the time I think I accepted that this was a peace I'd never known before, a light I'd never seen before, and it had a magnitude I can't explain and it also had its own form of magnetism on my soul. I felt a lot of love—love and peace. I felt tranquil, I felt wanted and accepted. I didn't feel judged in any way—I think whoever it was understood the situation.

I don't know what would've happened once I got right into that light, because as I got very close to it I heard a voice distinctly sing out, a very strong voice, "Go back!" (I think it was my younger brother's voice—we had been extremely close.) And then I sort of stopped and then I heard it again, "Go back!", really loud, but not scary, not angry. And I thought, "Well . . . that's what I'll do." I think I was on the edge, nearly there. I had no doubt that I only had to go just a little bit further and I would be amongst a lot of people that I hadn't seen for a while.

When I look at it now they must have thought, "Hey, this is the easy way out, mate—back you go!" It's like when you see a spirit level leveling out. Then I just started to slide back.

By this time I didn't know, but my sister had arrived. She was sitting on a little chair next to the bed. There was also a beautiful old priest. I couldn't believe it, he was over the top of me, anointing me, giving me the last rites. I looked at him and I wasn't scared. I saw my sister there and I sort of felt for her. And I woke up. At the time I smoked cigarettes, and I think my first words were, "Who's got a cigarette?" And the priest said, "I don't believe this." I can't remember exactly all the words he used but he said, "You're a very lucky man, very lucky—you're supposed to be dead."

After that they actually took me away to another hospital. It was quite an experience. One thing's for sure—I wasn't on the line when they rang the bell for pills! They made sure I got no pills whatsoever. And I was kept there until I got enough strength to get well again. By that stage I think I was about 145 pounds in weight—for six-foot-two, that's pretty light. I was in the hospital for about six weeks under observation.

I came out of the hospital very angry in a way, and I believe quite paranoid. I ended up on a drug which was injected into me every two weeks. I can't blame the doctor for that now, since he was the one who had to listen to my madness at the time. All I wanted was to find something that would nullify the fears. But I became very dependent on that drug. Coming off it, I used a hell of a lot of other drugs—you name it, I used it. It was a pretty big withdrawal actually. And I wasn't about to stop even then.

I didn't try to kill myself again. But it was very hard to put all that down. I'd been living for so long like that. I found that when the chemical substances were finally taken away from me, it was very hard to relate to people. The miracle of the situation, I feel, is for me to be sitting here now in good health talking about it.

It would've been about six months before I went into a detox, and then I went through shocking withdrawals. I found it very hard, mainly because I'd already seen two brothers die—the older one took his life through pills and my younger brother, who was only a year younger than me, died of three massive heart attacks in my sister's arms. (The same sister who was at the side of my bed.) I was in the middle of this and I thought, "Well, I don't think this is fair!" So I found it hard to get things together until I could let go of all that, and start again. Those withdrawals I had at that detox, I never want that again—acute paranoia, fears. So that's a chunk of my life, a small chunk.

I do find the whole experience hard to put into words. I don't think I've ever had so much peace in all my life. It wasn't like a dream at all. I mean if I *could* put it into words, it was like reality, but in a spiritual form. But it's something that's only happened once in my life. I mean, if anyone asked me in the street, I'd tend to shut off a bit about it. I just don't open up about it. I think most people would be very cynical about it. Although, come to think of it, once or twice I *have* related my experience to strangers. At one stage I used to work in welfare and sometimes I'd run across the odd rough diamond here and there, and if I thought there might be a chance it'd help, I'd share my experience with them.

While the experience was happening I had a sense of peace and calm, but later on I had a tendency to be sad, too. I realized how selfish I'd been with my daughter and all of those people I'd left behind. Now I feel a lot different—I've started thinking about other people instead of only myself.

It sure changed my ideas about death. By my religious conditioning I thought that if I didn't go to church or committed adultery, you name it, I'd burn in hell. Or if I was lucky I'd go to purgatory, and they'd cook me for a while, have a barbecue, or if I was a goody-goody, went to church every Sunday and wore the halo, I'd be going straight up to heaven, which I pictured as angels and all that. I worked on that assumption all the time, I rehearsed that. It's hard to get rid of when it's pumped into you. You see my mother was very religious—rosaries every night, nine o'clock Mass. That was all right for her. But when I look at the conditioning I copped over the years, I can see how it dragged me down.

But now I look forward to death, it's a pretty relaxed state. I look forward to catching up on friends. I don't think there'd be any hassles whatever, once you're over. But as far as details go, I'm of two minds about it. I don't know whether I'll be back again after I do die, to do another course of development or whatever, or whether I'll go into another sphere for untold time (since there is no time), and when my number comes up, maybe I'll end up in Boston somewhere or I'll end up in Russia—I'll come back as a Russian, or whatever. I tend to believe that more than anything. Yet, I don't feel like I'm going to be caned or anything.

I don't think I ever really thought about reincarnation before my experience, but now, especially lately, since my little boy's come along, I think it's beautiful. I feel a touch of my grandfather (who I never even met) in him. When he was five months old, we took him down to the opera house. I just felt like going down to hear some classical music, hear the orchestra down there. The woman outside was worried he might make a noise, but I said I felt very sure he wouldn't. And there he was, sitting up, watching the violins and frowning a bit. I just felt a bit of my grandfather coming through—he was a conductor. I felt a touch of him coming through, it was really remarkable. It really touched me.

I can't say I feared death before my experience, because I wasn't a responsible person, I was too junked out. I only ever thought about it much earlier, before I ever touched any drugs. But now when I think about it, I have an acceptance, an acceptance that I'm going to leave here one day, and also I think of the things that I'll leave behind. I always think of my daughter and I think of my little boy.

I suppose I had a funny concept of suicide because

as a child I lived a lot in fear of my father's aggression. And my elder brother committed suicide. He was quite a character and he'd done a lot of things in his life by the age of thirty. Anyway, he took an overdose. He'd been dead for five days when he was found. And before I decided to call it a day with my soul, I used to constantly think about my two brothers—I suppose there was an inclination to be with them. I thought, "What an easy way out." But now I wouldn't do it. I feel negative about it, I relate to it as a very negative thing to do. But still, if I hear other people saying that someone's jumped off the Gap, I relate exactly to that area of their mind where they're at, and it's frightening. It's frightening for me. Other people will say "they're crackers," but I just think to myself, "I know where they're at."

I'm not afraid around death now at all. After my experience I knew I was meant to come back for various reasons. One of these was to put in some energy to my mother, who was later to die of Alzheimer's disease. She was left on her own after my father died. Anyway, I was to be around, thank God, to see her die, to see how peaceful she was when she died. In the last couple of days she could see something beautiful and I related, I could relate to her facial expressions, and I could see in her eyes that she was happy. I'd go in there in the night and I'd feed her. I think, when I look back, it was lovely to be able to do that. It was lovely to be able to feel the emotion she was going through, beautiful to be there with her. The last time I saw her it was beautiful just to hold her (she was four stone [about fifty-five pounds] by that time) and to tell her how much I really loved her. She was just sitting still and smiling.

I think of the near-death experience as spiritual not religious, and even though I was spiritually bankrupt before, now I do feel very spiritual. I don't think it's ego saying that. I do feel spiritual, I have a lot more peace than I've ever had before. I don't get it every day, but I know how to adjust myself now, and what's good for me in that regard. I think, if anything, it's helped me center into a realization of what life and death's all about. I think, as I got well, it tuned me in to a spiritual way of being.

It has changed my outlook on religion a hell of a lot. I haven't got the guilt mechanisms anymore. They're gone. I don't go running down to confession every week. In fact I don't go to church at all, but I have an awareness that there's something around me all the time. I feel pretty safe.

I've lost that mechanism that used to press a button saying, "You must pray now," but I do pray in my own way. I just talk in the shower or something. I just thank my Higher Power that my mum's all right. I miss her a lot, but I know the other side of the coin is that she's most happy when she sees me happy. So sometimes I might also have a talk to her. It's just an awareness—it's terrific.

I've done a fair bit of meditation now. And sometimes I sit out in the sunroom with the sun on my face for an afternoon, and I feel part of the universe.

I've changed a hell of a lot. A lot of people I know are filled with the stresses of life, but I try not to let that sort of thing get to me. I use the Higher Power to nullify that sort of stress. I'm very excited about it—I can feel myself growing. There are people in the street now that don't even recognize me, which to me is a compliment. People have walked past me!

I'm pretty psychic now, too. Before, I'd have said it was rubbish, but now I'm very open to it. I sometimes know who's on the phone when it rings and I know when my sister's coming over. She only comes once in a blue moon, but I know when she's coming. I can pick it up. And a few weeks back I had a really strong feeling that something had happened to my daughter. I felt this really strong urge: ''How is she?'' Anyway, I got a letter saying she'd had a little accident on her bike. It was very strong, very strong.

I had [another] while I was on a bushwalk in a national park. I said to someone, ''I wouldn't be surprised if there was a snake down here,'' and sure enough there was a huge black snake—six foot. I was flabbergasted. I believe we can tune in to them. Sometimes on these nice sunny days I can go out the back and be eating an apple and I can see the sparrows and I can tune in to them, have a listen—it's really lovely.

Looking at it now, I take a more meaningful look at things and I make that a priority. It's never-ending work—I'm doing it all the time. It's the same with self-understanding and self-esteem—I'm working at it all the time, accepting different things about myself and doing something about them.

I now feel I have a life purpose. I feel I've got a lot to give, whether it be a smile or whether it be just conversation, or it's just a feeling I have that if someone wants me, I can help them. I've never had that before—I always felt useless. But now I've tapped another source and I know it's there, and I know it's there as long as I want it.

I like to have a nice attitude to people. I like to be as calm as I can around people, I like to give as much love as I can, and I like to give it to people who bother me! And that's a real turnaround for me. I used to be a very aggressive person, unbelievable aggression was locked inside—hate for myself and for other people.

At this point in time I don't want to work full-time. I have enough material things—I don't have to be surrounded by them. I haven't got a lot of money, but I've got enough to last me. I consider I've got too many other things in my life at the moment that take up the day. I like to go and visit people, I like to train about four or five times a week, to keep well, that gives me unbelievable energy—good energy. I like to be surrounded by nature, and I have my spiritual program and my little boy. Of course, some days are a bit ratty, but compared to before, there's no comparison—it's just black and white. I suppose it comes from knowing myself. I've been reborn. There's no doubt about it. I'm just grateful that it happened. I see myself as extremely lucky!

In myself I think it was a miracle that I was given another chance. So now I try to carry that with me and try to do the work.

VIRGINIA

I was first introduced to Virginia by her husband, and some weeks later I went to her comfortable inner-city house to do the interview.

The word that first comes to mind when I think of Virginia is intense. *She has an intensity about her that reveals, I believe, a wholehearted commitment to life and her life's work. There is an intensity of gaze coupled with an ardent drive to communicate her ideas. But she is also motherly in a way that is quite independent of biological birthing—she is caring, nurturing and, one has the impression, capable of completing whatever needs doing. Even when relaxed and laughing, her strong personality is still evident just beneath the surface. She is vibrant and short in stature, with shoulder-length, wavy blond hair and fair skin. She wears colorful Indian jewelry and clothes—floaty cheesecloths, cottons and silks—but there is nothing of the blissed-out New Ager about Virginia.*

Curled up on the couch with a cup of herbal tea on hand, we did the interview. Virginia was twenty-four at the time of her NDE and I spoke with her twenty years later, at which point she was director of a school of esoteric sciences and co-manager of their specialist bookshop.

I had what could be termed a nervous breakdown. There was a series of events which left me feeling there was no point at all in living. At that stage it seemed there was no reason to continue in this life. I'd been in a hospital for about three months and they'd given me shock treatment. (I didn't realize until later just how bad shock treatment is.) I was totally drugged out—I didn't know what was going on. I was just a complete mess. But all the time I'd had in the back of my mind that I did *not* want to live. I was just very cagey about it—I played it cool and did all the things they wanted me to do.

One afternoon they let me out and I went straight to a doctor and invented a story about getting married and having trouble sleeping. Of course he gave me sleeping pills, there was no problem with that. I then went and got the prescription filled. My intention was that this was going to be it, and nobody was going to know about it. So I went down underneath the Harbour Bridge, thinking nobody would find me there. I got a bottle of Coke and casually proceeded to take the pills, thinking, "This is it, *finita*!"

But I was found—I woke up in the hospital. I'd been out for quite a long time, they'd pumped my stomach and all the rest of it. I'd been lying there, shocked, and a nursing nun came and spoke to me. She was just trying to tell me all this stuff and I didn't want to know about it. I was thinking, "It hasn't happened again, I'm still here!" So I ripped out all the drips and things, signed myself out and demanded an ambulance to take me back to the other place around the corner. About ten o'clock that night I started to feel a bit strange, things started to get a bit hazy. They hadn't given me anything when I went back around there, but I could feel something strange was happening—my heart was just pounding. I'm sure the body had just had too much, it couldn't take any more. So then my heart apparently stopped and they had to give me adrenaline.

While they were doing that, of course, I was up on the ceiling watching them and I was thinking, "This is it, this is what I wanted. Great! Here I go, wherever I'm going." I'd never had any total understanding of the after-death states as I do now, but I always knew in the back of my head that there was something more, and that's why I wanted to go, because I knew it was better than what my lot had been till then. So I went down along the usual tunnel that people see and toward a luminous light. There is no way in the world I could possibly describe this light because it's just something that has to be experienced. And as I got closer to the light there was a mental projection being projected to me to say, "No, you have to go back, it is not your time." Then something happened—there was a realization within me that this really was death and I had to go back. Within that particular situation some sort of change occurred. From my previous mental attitude of not wanting to live, now something *made* me want to live. I *had* to live somehow. Something happened. I can't describe it in words, it's very difficult. I just knew that that was that. So I came back into my body and I started to breathe again.

The main thing I remember at that point was being somehow more alive than before. Before the experience I might as well have been dead, from one point of view. I had been drugged out for three months. There'd been so many negative things happening to me, that all the switches had been practically switched off. But afterward, something had happened—I was very fragile, but I felt better about myself.

The next day I signed myself out of the hospital and I never went back, I never looked back. I never went to have follow-up counseling or anything. I just "voom!", sort of took off from there. I didn't totally heal, obviously—I had to heal myself. I didn't want to know about any medication, about doctors. I didn't want to know about psychiatrists or anything like that. I just wanted to get on with things. Life itself was not particularly good at times, but that was my own fault.

But now, of course, I know why I wasn't allowed to die then—I had more work to do. My understanding now is that I came into incarnation, into this life, to serve, to serve humanity in my own small way. I don't mean to sound prideful at all, but I know now that if I had died then, maybe a word or a seed thought that I could now give to somebody, would not have been given. I would not have been able to fulfill the particular karma that I can now fulfill in this life.

I did not talk about the experience with anyone until many years later. The particular lifestyle I had at first after the experience was still very hedonistic. I traveled the world and experienced everything you could possibly experience. There wasn't the quality (or I didn't recognize the quality) in people, to be able to really talk about things like that. (The whole reason why I got into the situation in the first place was because I never spoke to people very much.) I might have mentioned it from time to time in a very flippant way, but it wasn't until seven or eight years ago that I was able to talk about it with people who understood. Even then I only told a few—usually people who started to talk to me about things like that themselves. Or people who may have been trying to understand something, and could be helped by my relating my experience to them in that context.

I didn't even read anything about it until about seven years ago. I found it interesting that everyone who has the experience describes more or less the same thing. They can't all be making it up!

Before the experience I sort of knew that there was something after death, but I didn't consciously understand what it was. There was a part of me—a little seed, shall we say—that was in me that couldn't see the logic of this being all there is. But as to having a complete understanding of that, I can't say that I did at the time. But now, from my own knowledge and from being with people who have since died, I believe that one leaves the physical body, that there is a thread, a consciousness thread that is snapped, and the person then goes through the states of consciousness, of awareness, that I now know to be called the planes of perception, for want of a better word. There are helpers that come to help the person as well.

I suppose I used to fear death—if I ever had an accident, there was that jolting of fear. There was an occasion many years ago when I went down to Hobart and crewed back on a yacht. We got caught at sea in a huge storm and went about a hundred miles off course. We had to take all the sails down and just let the sea take us. I was strapped downstairs in one of the bunks and I didn't want to be there, I wanted to be up on deck, but apparently that was the best place to be in case the boat went over. Yet even while that was happening, there was something within me that wanted to get on with it. I felt, "Okay, if I've got to go, let's do it *now* instead of dragging it out."

But now I don't think I have any fear of death at all, mainly because I have a greater understanding of leaving the body. From one point of view we are dead sometimes in this physical body. Yet when I think of others close to me, I sometimes fear the loss. Like my mother at the moment is very ill, and I get this sense of loss when I think of her going. It's not so much a fear. I certainly don't fear my own death.

I feel now, though, that suicide is pointless, absolutely pointless. I now believe that the karma of suicide is such that you've got to come back anyway, you've got to work it out eventually. But at the time I really wanted to do it. I didn't just try pills; I'd tried the wrists and all sorts of things. But now, it seems to me that was a different person. That person was so lost, in so much pain, and with so much anxiety, so inadequate because of the particular experiences that had happened, with no confidence and no self-esteem. Nothing really good had happened to that person—there might have been tidbits of things, but nothing that was really good.

Since the experience I've become quite interested in issues around death and dying. I've done classes on "Death, the Great Adventure" and I'm always attuned, so that if I know someone's dying, I do special meditations for them. Recently a friend died and we all felt him around for about a week. He was very joyous and we were all having meditation impressions of him. Within the same week another friend's mother died, so we called on him to help her. That's the sort of interest I have. The interest is in helping people to understand what death is really like.

Before the experience I was not at all religious or spiritually inclined—I'd spit at the thought of saying the words *Jesus Christ* or *God*. I was baptized a Roman Catholic, so at the age of seven I was sent along to have instruction in taking my first Holy Communion. They said something good was going to happen, and I was really looking forward to this. I was dressed in a beautiful little white dress and lovely veil and all the rest of it. I remember it so distinctly—I went up to the altar and innocently put out my tongue, and nothing happened! I couldn't believe it. Before that I used to be taken to church by my grandmother (who brought me up). I used to just sit there and look around and I used to think how ridiculous it all was—even at that small age. This continued right up to my teens. I could see the hypocrisy, particularly of the Roman Catholic religion, where you can do anything you like, you go along on a Saturday to confess the sins and all of a sudden on the Sunday it's all forgotten and you can start again. Today I excuse it away as the difference between Christian activity and church activity. But there was always that belief within in God.

What the experience did was to help me get on with things, instead of messing around and wasting time like I did. I still can't say that I achieved anything great after that. Initially it just made me go and experience more things, but it somehow allowed certain doors to open that seemed to be closed before. It wasn't till some years later that I found the path I'm on now, and when I found that path there was suddenly a recognition of what that experience had been and why it had happened.

Today I consider myself to be a humanitarian, I consider myself to understand the teachings of Christ and Buddha, and I believe that I'm just a younger sister of these two enlightened beings. My understanding of the Christ is that everyone has the potential to become Christ. Everyone can move into the same sort of path as did the Buddha. My belief is in the gnostic thread that has always existed.

I have many psychic experiences—all the time, every day (laughs). I did have some before, but I didn't know what it was—I thought everybody had that sort of thing.

Now I see quite a few things. In relation to the teachings I see lots of things in my meditations. I also get certain teaching communications through clairaudience.[8] My husband and I were experimenting with telepathy for a while, and I found that the facility is there for that, too. When I was in France some years ago, I had a lot of déjà vu experiences. I'd just be looking around and suddenly there would be a flood of recognition, a flood of experiences would come through to me.

My intuitive sense has also increased dramatically since the NDE. With meditation and a vegetarian diet, my mind is much clearer. Nowadays I can see auras, but sometimes I just pick up a person's vibration. I sometimes get impressions about other people's past lives, too. But it's not just for the personality to know of these past lives—it's purely for the service purpose. It is something that has been developing over time, and it's a cyclical thing. Sometimes a thought will pop into my consciousness about a person. Sometimes it's given to the person, sometimes it isn't. I find it's important to be very careful with things like that.

All these particular facilities that are developed upon the path, they can be used, but I am careful not to get too caught up in them. I now feel there's an overall plan and I'm just making myself open to that plan. I know that I get impressions from my soul and I try to be as open as I can for the soul to impress upon me the right decisions.

In the past, life was one continual round of parties, theater, lots of dope, a complete pursuit of "having a good time." Now the best way to describe my lifestyle would be to go through my week and look at what actually happens. Three days a week I'm permanently in the bookshop, Tuesday and Wednesday nights I'm generally at the school—one night I might be giving a lecture, the other night I might be helping out. All the time within that I'm open to people who come in for counseling purposes. On Thursday I'm usually doing domestic tasks or running around doing different things. Thursday night I baby-sit, because we have a child in the household and she's lovely. On Friday night there's a class again. The weekends I spend with my husband and Sunday night is for meditation. My life is very full. In addition to all that, there are my own studies and my own preparations for class. I also like to paint, I like to do something creative, put jewelry together, things like that. In our household we like to spend a lot of time at home. We are all vegetarian and lead a meditative lifestyle. We consider ourselves a family, we pool all our resources, so we are really a small community in the city.

This is very different to how it used to be. In the past I only had lots of short-term relationships. When I say I was hedonistic, I was the particular generation I was. The old pendulum had swung the other way. We just did what we wanted. I just did what I wanted, I had no morals. If I wanted sex, I had sex, I just did it. Again I see it as a sort of karmic balance, I sort of understand why. My teacher once said to me, "The whole thing about being in these bodies is to experience." I did it for sure! (laughs).

I think I have a better understanding of myself now and I can accept my lot. The reason why I had such low self-esteem was I couldn't accept my upbringing. I could not accept the family in which I was born. I could not accept it, I did not accept it, I rejected it completely. Now I can accept it, now I accept my mother and have a genuine love for her, which of course reflects back on me. I feel I have a better self-esteem than I did have. I suppose I'm kinder on myself than I was before, but I'm still a bit too hard on myself, more than I should be at times, but I'm still working on it.

For the last eight years or so, there have been a lot of changes. No alcohol, no cigarettes—I smoked for twenty-three years! No alcohol, no cigarettes, no drugs, no sex or rock and roll (laughs). Maybe a little bit of rock and roll.

Today I try to be as open as I can to people. I find that I am much more forthright, that I'll say something now, whereas in the past I probably wouldn't have. At the same time I am more compassionate—I also understand when not to say anything. I suppose I'm more sensitive.

Now my priority is to be as useful as I can to those around me, and I suppose I'd like to be as content as I can within the situation in which I find myself. I like art, I like walking in the botanical gardens, I appreciate good music, and books of course. Obviously, working in a bookshop, I don't get a lot of time to read, but I get to look at a lot of books.

There are many social issues that concern me. I used to march for peace, but now I don't feel we can have peace in the climate that exists in the world today. I don't wish to sound negative toward those who genuinely believe we can work for peace, but I believe we can't possibly hope to have peace while materialistic views still exist in the world. We have to have genuine change before peace can happen. How can we think about peace when all around us, in our own city, there are things like homeless children? I believe we can work best for peace from the inside out. Education is my work toward peace—trying to change the values of people. Teaching people to appreciate that there is more to life than a three-dimensional view of things, that there is more to life than football, that there is more to life than that narrow frame of reference—to widen their horizons. I don't wish to sound airy-fairy about this because I genuinely believe that it will happen.

But I know I have to make decisions. How can *I* help within these parameters? There's a mantra which we say every day which is ''The Great Invocation,'' and we invoke light, love and power to come down to the planet to heal the planet as a whole. That might seem like a small thing, but it's something I can do to make a difference, that and the education thing. That's the way I do it. I can't do everything—as an individual I'm limited. But I just feel so strongly about so many things. This is one of the lessons I'm learning within myself—not to feel so strongly, not to feel so passionate about things, not to go off in a tantrum, but to try to be detached from them, and then act.

But above everything, I now accept that I have a genuine need to contribute. I now know that I have a place in this world and that I can be of service. I never had that before.

ROBERT

While traveling in Queensland conducting interviews with near-death experiencers, my husband and I stopped at a quiet coastal town. We were to stay there for a few days so that I could interview two NDErs, and then have a short rest before setting off back south again. In town one day my husband was asked casually whether he was on vacation, and he replied, "Not exactly. I'm accompanying my wife while she does her research."

"What's the research about?"

"Near-death experiences. Do you know what they are?" A shocked silence.

"I've had one of those!"

And so it went on for some minutes of animated conversation.

The next day my husband and I visited Robert in his trailer at a local trailer park. Robert is an invalid on disability, a big man with graying hair, slightly stooped and walking with some difficulty because of problems with his hip. He has a gentle manner and smiling eyes. While we sat in the annex of his trailer sipping tea, a couple of his friends arrived and were introduced. As it turned out, one of these friends also had had a near-death experience! After a while I began the interview in the presence of this very attentive audience.

Robert was forty-four years old at the time of his experience, and our meeting took place nine years later.

At the time of his suicide attempt Robert had been drinking heavily and was in a state of severe depression.

I had been living in England for many years where I worked as a residential child-care worker. I hadn't had a drink for twenty-five years, but after I got back to Australia I started drinking again—I was very, very depressed at the time. This day I blew my side out with a shotgun. I was home in bed when I did it—my mother woke me up that morning and I pulled the trigger as she tried to wake me.

The next thing I remember is looking down in the operating room, down on my body, with the surgeons around, and I distinctly knew, I knew it was me. I thought, "That's me. They're wasting their time, I'm not going back." And I can remember sort of drifting away from the body. At the same time I could hear the doctors saying, "I think he's going, he's gone!" And I thought, "Well, they're right, I've gone, I'm finished, I've got to go," and that's when I sort of felt this drifty feeling, it felt good to be going up.

I was trying to get to a distant light that I could see. It was a brilliant light of some sort, and I wanted to get to it, but I could feel this tug, tugging me back. And then I distinctly remember a voice saying, "Well, Robert, you're not finished yet—you have to go back. You're not ready, you're not finished with what you have to do." That was the impression I got, those sort of words. I tried my hardest to pull toward the brilliant light. I could see it in front of me. It was just a massive brilliance, a brilliant sphere, and I could feel that that's where I wanted to go. But after I heard the voice, I can remember coming back, and as I was coming back I could even sort of feel myself coming down toward my body. And then I remember waking up in the intensive-care unit sometime later.

I must admit after it happened I thought perhaps it

might have been the depression that had something to do with the vision, but then I felt it couldn't have been that because it felt so vivid and so good.

I even spoke to the doctor about it, and that's when he told me they'd declared me dead on the table. I had two sets of operations at the time and he'd supervised both of them. He said, "There must be some purpose. We were amazed that you lived because technically you should have died with the injuries you had. You must have been given another chance. You must have been given another chance to do something."

I said, "Well, I don't want it!" Because I didn't want to live then, I was still in a depression. But that incident, whatever it was, was still vivid, and to me it was a happy experience. It wasn't a bad experience in any way. I was a bit disappointed because I couldn't go, but then I was happy to be back in one way and unhappy in another way.

While I was still in the hospital I spoke to a couple of doctors about it. But then I had to go to the psychiatric section because I was still very depressed. There I spoke to two of the psychiatrists about it. One psychiatrist pooh-poohed the idea, but the other psychiatrist said he'd heard of similar experiences and he was keen to talk to me about it. We did speak about it and he asked me what I felt about it. He said, "Doesn't it make you feel better about your depression, doesn't it help you get out of it?" At the time I had to say no, because I wasn't very clear. But toward the end, when I stopped getting so depressed, I did respond better to him. I became aware then that he must be right, the feeling I had must have been a true feeling. Because until that particular time I wasn't sure whether it was an actual experience over the operating room or whether it was just something in my imagination, due to everything else. But he pointed out how it tied in with what happened in the operating room, and with what the surgeon said about being clinically dead and then suddenly rallying round. And he said, "We've had this happen before." He said, "It's happened a few times—we think they're gone and then suddenly the patient rallies round."

Since then I've come across a few things about it. I haven't gone out of my way to read anything in particular, but I've picked a few things up, an article here or there in magazines.

Before the experience I was afraid of dying, but I didn't really think much about what happened at death. Now I think it's just another step to something. Now I have no fear of dying, I have no actual fear of death. Death doesn't worry me in the slightest, because now I have the feeling that death's like birth. Birth is an experience we come through, and death's another experience to go through. But I must admit a few years back, before this experience, it used to worry me how I died. Even when the wife died (she died from cancer), I was very worried about that. Death seemed to be a final thing then. But now it doesn't appear that way to me. It's just another door to open up and to go through.

Now I'm glad I didn't commit suicide, that I didn't die, but if you'd asked me a month after it happened, I was still very full of anger and didn't want to live. I feel that someone who wants to commit suicide must be very deeply depressed to believe they have to do that—I know I was. I feel very sorry for people who do commit suicide, but I suppose if someone does it, they must have some deep reason and desperate need to do it. We just haven't found the right way of helping these people.

But when I look back on it now, that vision I had over the operating room did help me to come back to myself again afterward. It was a good experience, it wasn't a horrible experience, it was a beautiful feeling. There was no fear, no ill feeling, it just felt fantastic.

• • •

I think of it as a spiritual experience, not religious. I've never been very religious, but when I was about twenty-one I became very involved in my church, the Presbyterian church, and the Christian faith, but now my mind is open. I'm not a firm believer in any particular religion. I don't think Christianity is the whole answer. I think every faith on this earth stems from the one thing, a universal thing. My thinking on that is fairly open. I never go to church now, but I meditate most mornings—I do my readings and then I have a particular thought that I meditate on for the day. I suppose subconsciously I pray—I give thanks for the way things have gone through the day, and that sort of thing, just a silent prayer within myself.

I think I'm slowly becoming more spiritual. I now have a greater awareness of myself and my own spirituality, if that's the right way to put it, than I did before. In the last twelve months I've become even more aware of that sort of thing, and the experience has been a lot in my thoughts. I feel more spiritual within myself, I feel a change within myself, but it's not a religious change. I'm not a fanatic religious person, I don't go out and preach this or that. Whatever a person believes in, I accept that that's their way.

I am a believer in reincarnation now. I already did have a bit of a belief when I was younger—I used to read books on reincarnation, but I had no strong feelings about it. Now it sort of ties in with my feeling that death is just another experience to go through. Whether it leads to reincarnation or what, I do feel that death is not the ultimate experience. I feel that we have further experiences to go through.

I have quite a few psychic experiences these days. I sometimes get the feeling that something's going to happen, and then when it happens, it's no surprise. I had one just last week with a friend. I knew full well inside myself that Frank was going home to die. I just said, "I don't think I'll be seeing you again." And he said, "I don't think so either." It wasn't a surprise to me at all when I heard on Wednesday that he'd died.

Years before, I had a similar experience when the wife died. I knew she was going and I went to her and said, "Well, I think you're going now, Bette." And she said, "Yes." I said, "I'm very glad that it's gone so quickly for you," because she suffered from cancer. But it was very hard.

As a child I had a slightly different sort of experience. I can distinctly remember when I was about fifteen, my grandmother died, and I remember her coming to me to say good-bye. And shortly after, the phone went at our place and I said to Mum, "That's uncle ringing up, Grandma's just died," and sure enough Grandma had just died, about three or four minutes before. I didn't think much of that, you know, I just had that feeling that she'd gone—we were very close.

I'm quite aware of my dreams, and sometimes I get the feeling I've been somewhere, visited some friends—an astral sort of thing. I've sometimes woken up and thought to myself, "Oh yes, I was just talking to so and so, I'll hear from them soon." And I do. In other dreams I dream I'm somewhere and then later I suddenly find I'm there. I might have had the dream ages ago, and suddenly I'll see the thing that I've dreamed about, and I think, "Well, that's funny." It's like a dream coming true. I feel like I've been there and experienced it before. I sometimes get the same sort of feeling about people. I feel I've met this person somewhere before, but I haven't, as far as I know. I feel I know them well but I don't, if you can understand what I mean.

These days I seem to be more aware, more ready to accept things and people, as they are. It used to be very hard for me to get on with a lot of people. I was very argumentative, picking faults and deliberately going out of my way to draw anger. But now I try to look for the good in people, and when I find it I try to bring it out. If I can help them, I will. If they want help, I'm there. Now I enjoy working with the elderly—that's why I go up to the care center—it's for old people who are stuck at home and wouldn't otherwise get out. Even though lately I've also been going up there to get massaged, I enjoy going there because I enjoy working with the elderly people.

I am also a firm believer in the hospice system, in the right of the elderly to die the way they wish, with dignity. That's something I have given a lot of thought to—especially when I think of the wife's death and the way my stepfather went. People should have the right to die in the manner they wish—and that's with dignity. I am a firm believer now that if someone's dying from a terminal illness, they shouldn't be allowed to suffer. I think there is enough to suffer without having to suffer a painful death. I think the right should be there to terminate if they so wish, and that's a different thing to suicide. But I wouldn't like to be the one to make that decision.

The most significant change for me has been getting more understanding—self-understanding and an awareness that there is something I've still got to do. What it is, I still don't know yet—perhaps save lives, try to help other alcoholics, it could be that. Whatever it is, I don't know, but I'm not worried about it. Whatever it is, it will come to me eventually. It's just a feeling that my life is not finished yet—there's still some purpose to fulfill.

At Christmastime I was in the hospital to have a hip replaced. I developed a bad clot in the lung, and they put me in intensive care. Just prior to going into a coma I remember the doctor saying, "Well, Robert, we've only got a few short minutes to try and do something with you, because you're clotting very bad in the lungs and you could go.'' And I said, ''Well, I don't think so, I don't think they want me yet. I haven't done what I've got to do.'' I said the Serenity Prayer and then went into a coma. I woke up the next day.

I think it has taken some time to realize, it's taken a while for it to really sink in, but I think the changes in my life since the experience have been very much for the better. There's been a real personality change. I understand myself better these days. I now have a spiritual awareness of myself and it seems to get stronger each day. It's funny, it's hard to describe, but I feel I'm getting stronger in it every day. It's just as if I'm growing again. I feel as if I'm spiritually growing now where before I'd stopped. I don't know if I sound silly, but that's how it is for me.

CHAPTER 3

Frightening Experiences

For as long as modern near-death research has been conducted there has been a curiosity about the apparent lack of so-called negative stories among contemporary accounts. In the past, for instance in medieval times, reports of otherworldly visions—"educational tours" of the otherworld, including journeys through the terrors of hell—were well-known, since they were very effectively exploited by the church for its own purposes. The recounting of a vision often became a collaborative effort as the reticence of the visionary was overridden to develop the story into a convincing conversion narrative.[1] Such stories were lucrative for the church, as they served to confirm the need for expensive funeral rites and intercessory Masses on behalf of the dead. Even earlier, Plato recounted the story of Er, a soldier who came back to life on the funeral pyre twelve days after he was killed in battle.[2] During his time in the other world Er was told that he was to be a messenger to men, and therefore was ordered to "listen to and watch all that went on in that place." Upon his return to life he told of all he had witnessed—the punishments and penalties as well as the rewards.

In more recent times, this sort of story has been rare. Raymond Moody reported in the 1970s that nobody had ever described to him a state resembling "the archetypical hell,"[3] and Kenneth Ring[4] noted that there was a total absence of hellish experiences among his many cases of NDEs. The work of other researchers has similarly revealed that such cases are in fact extremely unusual.

Of negative reports that have surfaced in contemporary times, Maurice Rawlings's work is perhaps the best known, taking as it does an extreme view. In 1978 Rawlings presented the thesis that hellish NDEs are simply repressed. Arguing as he does, however, from a "born-again" Christian perspective with the clear agenda of proving to readers the existence of hell and therefore the need to be "saved," his presentation is questionable. Somewhat more convincing were the six NDEs recorded by Margot Grey, five of which included elements of panic, fear, isolation or desperation, and one of which featured hell-like imagery.

More recently, P.M.H. Atwater discussed "unpleasant" NDEs in an editorial for the *Journal of Near-Death Studies,* and an article by Bruce Greyson and Nancy Evans-Bush, which surveyed fifty reports of distressing NDEs that were collected over a nine-year period, was published in *Psychiatry.* Greyson and Evans-Bush identified three types of distressing experience: the first (and by far the largest group) included experiences similar to the usual NDE but which for some reason were interpreted as frightening; the second (smaller group) revealed the experience of a void; and the third (the smallest group) included typical hellish images.

When giving public talks, I am frequently asked whether I have ever come across anyone who has recounted a negative experience. In response I always have to relate that among the hundreds of near-death experiencers I have personally spoken with, I have only come across two who described anything that could be even vaguely construed as having a frightening element, and in neither case did the person concerned think of their experience as being "negative." This chapter will present the stories of these two NDErs—Alexandra, whose experience included hell-like imagery before unfolding in a typically positive way; and Cass, whose experience appeared outwardly to have many of the usual positive NDE features and yet was experienced by her as frightening.

Cass

I first met Cass when she came to my home with another producer to talk about a possible television show. Clearly she was outgoing, had a wide smile and sparkling eyes, but the thing that struck me most about her at the time was her extraordinary level of vitality—I remember at one point we were all dancing and whirling around my living room. Later, as we sat overlooking the ocean, conversation turned to psychic phenomena and spiritual concerns. I talked about my NDE and she revealed that she also had had one during an operation after breaking her neck doing aero-

bics. When I began my doctoral research the following year I immediately thought of her and made contact again.

Cass was forty-seven at the time of her NDE and I spoke with her two years later, in her upper-floor apartment, situated on a hillside with a distant view of the sea.

I had my experience as I was coming out of my second operation. I had broken my neck, and in the first operation, the year before, I had had a fusion of the spine. Unfortunately that wire broke, and within ten months I had to have it fused a second time. I really should have died.

The experience that I had was of just traveling so fast through black, and it *was* black. I can't explain the black—it was bright, bright black. And in the beginning it was just incredible. There was a big, big light, and then that opened up and *whoosh,* I went through into millions and billions of tiny little lights. They weren't stars, they were like lights, little white lights. And I was just *whooshing* down and then I heard somebody saying to me, "Come on, get up. You're going home, there's nothing the matter with you. Come on, get up—there's nothing the matter with you, you're going home." And then I heard a sound like big cymbals clashing, I felt that there was something cymbal-like in front of me, and I heard somebody say, "She's dying, she's dead." And that was that.

I was trying to say, "I'm all right." I was trying to talk and say, "I'm all right, there's nothing the matter with me." At the same time this voice kept booming, "Get up, you're all right, you're going home."

That was my experience, it was just incredible. I thought it was the voice of my doctor, because that's exactly what it sounded like. When I questioned him about this later, he said that it wasn't his voice, he wasn't talking to me at all. But apparently my heart had stopped.

I will never forget that experience. It's changed my whole life. I couldn't say it was magnificent, but I could say that it was overwhelming, it was frightening. It was frightening because I didn't know where I was going. It was not a splendid thing for me at all. The noise of the cymbals was incredible—it was like it was right in front of my face, but all I could see was the black, and these lights. I felt frightened—it was just the speed and the blackness. And I couldn't see myself but I could *feel* I was in there going through this, and it was so fast. But as I say, it was bright, bright black and these lights, they were static, but there were thousands and millions of them. And I was *whooshing* through all this. It was frightening.

I felt I was struggling to let people know I was all right. I had the sense that I was trying to tell them I wasn't dead, that I was all right, but my mouth wouldn't open. It was strange because I had thought I was going to die under the first operation. They kept telling me that I was facing instant death continually. And there I was the second time thinking, "Well, this is it. I'm dead. I knew I was going to die, now I'm dead." I was sort of accepting it, but part of me was fighting it. I was very frightened actually, because I didn't know what was happening to me. It was an unknown. I kept thinking, "What's it going to be like? Where am I going?" It was just myself and those thoughts. That's all I can say—it was just hideous really. It was hideous for me, and I will never forget it. Never.

I wanted to come back to my body. I was really struggling. And when I did get back it was incredible. I remember that there was somebody near me, a nurse or a doctor. And it was just a huge relief. It was like being back in another world. I then heard somebody talking to me and I realized it was one of my very dear friends.

I remember later asking my doctor what he'd been doing, had he been clashing anything, did he have cymbals or anything like that. And he said, "Oh, don't be silly. What would I be doing with cymbals?"

I think I had that experience to make me aware that I was a very, very selfish person. I'd never before thought of myself as a selfish person. There was nothing that I wanted—I had a great career, my life had been good. But over the previous year there'd been big problems in my marriage. My husband and I had been together for nearly twenty years, and I put that at risk! Now when I look at it I think, "Why did I do that?" I could never answer that. Everything's okay now—I have a really happy relationship. My home life is very, very content. I do more for my husband now than I ever did before.

I think I had the experience so that I would look fairly at my life. And that's exactly what's happened—I have become a better person, a nicer person. It really did change me. I'm not selfish at all now. I really feel very, very sorry for people who aren't aware of other people's needs. I give myself much more to people now, much more to things that are important. I cannot stand small talk, I can't stand anything that's not positive—I'll tolerate it but I don't like it.

Since then a lot of doors have opened up for me, good things are coming to me. I've changed jobs—now I'm running a couple of businesses. I'm in health and nutrition, and caring for other people. And I'm so happy, every day is a joy to me, *every* day! If somebody complains about the rain, I say to them, "Well, why are you worried about it? You're alive, and it's a terrific world!" And here I am walking around with a great big bunch of wire in my head—I should never have lived. And I think it is probably to help people, that's the feeling I get.

At that particular time I was almost finished writing a novel. I made that experience the last chapter—it was basically about my life anyway. But I just don't have any desire to write anymore, even to finish it. All ego has gone, all ego has gone in the sense of wanting to outdo somebody else. All career ambition has gone, and because that's gone, everything happens for me.

I've only tried to tell a few close friends about the experience, because I feel it's very private. It's something people are inclined to laugh at. Not that I give a damn about that, but it's just that I feel it's something very intimate between myself and God. I firmly believe that. I felt that experience was totally spiritual. Totally. It was frightening, but thinking about it now, I wish I could go back, just to inquire a little bit more about it.

I didn't have any interest in death or dying at all before my NDE. But being a Roman Catholic, even before the experience I already did believe in life hereafter. I still believe that our souls go somewhere and we are reunited with all those that have gone before us and we live forever. I'm not as frightened of death now. It's not that I want to die, but now that I've had that experience, I wouldn't be frightened because I'd sort of have some idea of what's at the end of it.

I was born Roman Catholic. My mother was the choir lady, very, very religious, we went to Mass every Sunday, and all that. After I left home I kept going until I was about twenty-four, and even then I'd go now and again. I would always go when I was in trouble—whenever I was feeling really down, I'd turn to religion to get me out of trouble. But since the experience my religion is much more important to me. Now on Sundays I get up and go to Mass, and I think I've got to because I think any day could be the end and I want to be prepared. Every day I pop into the church and have a visit. And I pray. I fall asleep praying, and always say a quick little prayer when I wake up in the morning. But now I've even started to look at the Bible—I'd never ever picked up a Bible in my life before. Now I try to read a passage every day.

I believe people can embrace any religion they like, because I think we all believe in the one God. It just happens I was born into a Catholic family, and reared in a convent. I could never ever get away from it, because I am so indoctrinated. I suppose many people *have* broken away from the Catholic religion, but I will never doubt it, never. I never ever doubt the teachings, I believe they've come straight down from God. I don't like the modernization of some things in my religion, but I suppose they're trying to reach out to a different generation.

I suppose I've always believed in psychic things, too. I've sat in a church and felt the presence of my mother there. And when my mother died I went near the coffin, I had her rosary beads in my hands, and they just snapped! It wasn't my imagination. I was a little kid, I was talking to her and crying and her rosary beads just snapped, the wire broke. I only ever told my grandmother that.

I've always felt somehow that I've been here before, that I have been another person. I get the strong feeling that I lived in the Victorian era, and anyone coming to my place would see that I can't stand anything modern, I cannot stand anything that is cold. I love velvets, I love old-world things. I always feel most happy and comfortable in those surroundings.

I'm also very clairvoyant, but that's something that I keep very much to myself. My experiences have been with finding things, especially animals. I've found many, many lost animals—I've actually seen them. One experience was with a very old friend of mine, a very old lady who'd lost her beautiful white cat. She was so distressed. As soon as she told me, I just got this quick flash, and I said, "It's all right, I can see it, and it's not far from here, in the schoolyard.'' She went over, and that's where the cat was. I've had many experiences with animals—that's only one of them. I sometimes wonder why, although I know I do have an affinity with animals, I do love them. I'm always feeding little strays, taking them in, looking after them and getting help for them.

But I've also had experiences with people where I can feel that they're telling lies, or that they haven't been where they say—I can see them in other places. I have a friend at the moment who's in dreadful trouble—he got sacked yesterday. He called me this morning and said, ''I'm just so frightened.'' I said, ''Don't be frightened, because everything's going to be all right.'' I can see that next week he's going to walk into something else. I feel really strongly about it.

My whole personality's changed since my experience. I'm a calmer, quieter person. I am still gregarious, but I don't show it as much now. I listen to other people. I never used to listen to other people at all.

I'm never lonely anymore, I no longer feel isolated. I have so many things in my life now to interest me. I love my own company. I love my little study and I can stay in there all day. I love my home, I feel it around me—it's quiet and nice, and good and clean (laughs). I sometimes get a little bit annoyed when the phone rings—sometimes it seems it never stops ringing—that's my health-and-nutrition business. I just go a hundred miles an hour now, but every day, when it comes five o'clock, I stop, I put the phone on the answering machine, and just have some time with myself. Life's beautiful. I'm so happy, it's joyous (laughs). I feel I could just cry out to the world that I've been uplifted, I have honestly been lifted.

Nothing worries me now because I know everything will be okay. It is just wonderful. I say to my doctor, I don't know how I do all these things in the day. I am up at five-thirty in the morning, I have a cup of tea and feed the birds. As soon as it's light I stick on an old tracksuit and walk the dog, and everything gets done. At a quarter to nine I'm ready for that phone to ring or whatever. But it's so easy! I don't get flustered, and that's exactly how it's been since that experience. Just wonderful! God is always there to help me. I've sometimes asked my mother for help, too. I think that God gives us these people, these guides or guardian angels, to help us. I believe that, I really do.

Now I always have a feeling of well-being, that everything is all right, that everything is going to be great. Deep down I think maybe I've been through all those things to get to this point. I believe we've got to earn love, we've got to earn respect, and I think now I've earned love. I don't mean love as in "passion," I just mean *love.*

I found that in death, you face it alone, completely alone. I realized that the very first day when they said, "Look, you're facing instant death. You're not going home, your neck's broken." I was curled up in the spinal ward and that's when I started to look at all this: "What's it going to be like? What's going to happen to me?" And I started to pray to God, and asked for the Holy Spirit to enter into me to give me strength. And a big calmness came over me, it really did. That was wonderful. But I felt I was still on my own. It doesn't matter if you've got a lover or a husband, or five thousand kids, you're on your own and you face it alone. But my husband was there morning, noon and night, and I thought to myself, "Gosh, did I have to go through all this to find this out?" My husband was the only person who stood by me when I broke my neck. That was incredible, I'll never forget him for that. Our relationship is much stronger now.

I've also become very, very close to my sister since

the experience. Before I didn't like her because she just didn't fit into my social set. I was a terrible snob!

I was in show business and it's a very cliquey area. I don't miss it at all. After my experience I couldn't get out of show business quickly enough. I just didn't want any part of something so material, so phony. I didn't want to be mixed up with those people anymore. I mean, I've still got lots of friends in TV who are like us, and I still see those people. But my old TV friends—they were so ambitious, so hard, you know? I was just so glad to get in my car and get away from all that bitchiness, all that nothing. And I thought, it's almost like having a secret, which you can't pass on to somebody else.

I like to be with my sort of people now. I find that I am coming to be with my sort of people more and the others are going. I'm not two-faced anymore. Now I'm in health and nutrition, and I care for people and help people. I mean, it's a business, but it's wonderful to see someone losing weight or somebody gaining weight, or somebody's blood pressure coming down. And, you know, there's a lovely feeling of respect for people. I'm studying and training all the time, and that's been fantastic for me.

Also after the accident I enrolled at the university to do a B.A., majoring in drama. I got right up to the end of the year, but I just couldn't go on because I got too busy with all my other things. I went to orientation and was out on campus. It was something that I had to experience, and I did it. There I was—an external mature-age student, and I found it very exhilarating.

I'm very energetic, I still do lots of things. I'm much more compassionate and caring for others' needs, but I'm also doing more things now for my own inner satisfaction. It's important to me to do the right thing. I can't tell lies now, I even find that I don't blaspheme as much! I just try to be a really nice person.

I really wish a lot of people could have the experience—it would change the world! I just wish the whole world could feel the way I feel.

Alexandra

The year I began my research, I heard that Alexandra had recently talked about her NDE to a meeting of the Jung Society. I also learned that she was to run a day-long workshop on death and dying in an idyllic setting on a clifftop high above the coast just south of Sydney. Naturally, I signed up for it.

The workshop was a very moving experience for me, but it also gave me the opportunity to get to know Alexandra better than would otherwise have been possible in an interview setting. I found her to be a warm, gentle, softly spoken person. She had a simplicity and directness that I found very appealing, and within the context of the workshop it became clear that she was both highly skilled and empathic in her work with the participants.

The following week I visited her at a friend's house, where she was staying until returning to her private practice in the United States. I was fortunate that she was able to fit me into her busy schedule—she ate breakfast while we talked. Alexandra was twenty-nine years old at the time of her NDE and we spoke twenty years later.

It seemed to happen in stages—it wasn't just one thing. I was very aware that the staff were terribly worried about me. This was five days postoperative—I'd had my left kidney removed and was suffering from a bloodstream infection. They were watching me closely, they were coming in and out and I was having blood transfusions. I was sort of groggy and delirious and in a lot of pain, and they'd just given me more shots. I was aware that I was more and more out of my body, and it sort of bothered me a bit at first, because I thought, "Maybe I'm dying!" I'm not sure how much I really knew, but I knew I was on the dangerously ill list, and I knew that the only people who were allowed to see me were my immediate family—and they were too upset to come in! So I really got the feeling that it was kind of bad (laughs).

And then I was aware that I could overhear things at the nurses' station from my bed. And in retrospect I realized that I had been watching part of the operation. I remembered watching them open me. And then I think I must have passed out for a while, but I did remember which nursing staff were there and—you know, they're all dressed up—you have to really know their eyes, to know who it is. I told them later, and they were so shocked they said, "But you were asleep!" And I said, "No, I saw you there." So there was this increasing number of little journeys out of the pain and out of the worry.

I remember that every time the doctor came in he sort of had a little frown and was very silent. He was a very nice person and had a lovely bedside manner. He was the surgeon, but he was something more of a physician. I realized I was picking up everybody's worries, and I began to realize that what I wanted to tell them was, "Hey, when I'm out of my body, I just feel great!"

I remember sort of rolling and skipping and flying and moving very freely, and I kept thinking, "Wouldn't it be nice to do that again?" (laughs). There was that split memory of in-body/out-body and I remember at one stage sort of skipping down into a little courtyard near the chapel, and it was a nice place. I remember later trying to visit there again in my out-of-body state, when it occurred to me that I might have some trouble if they shut the window and I couldn't get back in (laughs), so I decided I'd better just look at it and not go so far.

One day, when my vital signs must have really been bothering them, they brought in a priest to anoint me and I thought, ‘‘Oh, things must be pretty bad! (laughs). What is it they're not telling me?’’ Those thoughts were very alive in me. I remember him getting so far as offering me the host, the bread, and he had the chalice in his hand and he suddenly just fainted, and I remember thinking, ‘‘Oh, but I never got it—will I go to hell or something?’’(laughs). He just blacked out and someone came in and helped him out. He just sank to the floor.

I do remember trying to comfort my mother in that out-of-body stage—I didn't literally go home to her, but I remember just seeing her sitting at home, and feeling how sad she was and how really grief-stricken she was that I might go before her. That was very poignant. She had cancer herself at the time, and my dad had died a year before. So my sister was just desperate, and my brother was in such pain! He did come to the hospital twice, but then he just couldn't proceed up the stairs—his legs just gave out. His wife's father was in the hospital at the same time, so the only visitors I had were my sister-in-law's father, the chaplain who came to anoint me (he wasn't too helpful) and one friend, a very, very nice man, just a very dear person who brought me my favorite flowers several times. And I remember he had such a feeling of light around him. He had fairly recently buried his father and I could just feel this love coming out of him.

But the final big experience was on that fifth day, sometime in the afternoon. I just felt myself right up on the ceiling, and they were talking about changing the intravenous or something, and there was a little kind of conference. Shortly thereafter, I felt myself falling into an abyss. And it was a kind of, not flying, this was falling, this was out-of-control motion. It was very, very terrifying and seemed to go on for a long time. I felt like there was slush around me and "gush," and there was no air. It was moist and dark and there were sort of nasty shapes and smells. I visualized I was falling into some awful pit, but it was quite large and there were no walls, and there were no parameters and there was less and less light. And then it was just pitch-dark.

I remember praying my heart out that I wasn't just going to be lost in space or the universe. I felt like I was falling into hell. I felt that this must be hell and that I would perish, or would even be eaten, or go to ooze, or I would just die. Not just die, I'd be obliterated! It was the most awful feeling. That was one of the most frightening things I think that's ever happened to me. I was so alone. And anyway I did, at that moment of what you would call absolute terror and despair, of course cry out, rather helplessly, but I cried out. And I also remember I heard nothing, not in this part of the experience.

But I finally seemed to land and what I landed in was like the size of a huge sort of bed, but it wasn't a bed, it was two large arms. And I did get the feeling of, "Oh, don't forget, underneath are the everlasting arms."[5] And I just felt that this was about as underneath as I could go (laughs). I felt myself being held. I felt like I was being told, "You're a child of God." And soon after I began to hear my grandmother's voice. I hadn't ever heard my grandmother's voice in real life, but she was speaking to me in French, and I understood her perfectly. I do understand some French, but I understood it better than usual, and then gradually I saw her. She had a body of light, she definitely was not just flesh and blood, but she was very warm. She had a body but she seemed to be full of love, and that's what I'm calling light—it felt very warm and radiant and bright and lovely. Light was coming from her. She said to me, "You can choose whether to live or die."

Suddenly the seriousness of it really hit me, not only

at a gut level of terror, but at a mind/heart level. I thought, ''Oh, this is for real!'' There was no sense of play about it. I mean, before that, the out-of-body thing was very playful. When I heard her voice—''You can choose whether to live or die''—it was just like a knife, and I thought, ''God, how can I choose? I don't know, I don't know about these things.'' I didn't even know you could choose that. I can remember thinking how I'd never thought about that question. At that point I felt as if she was holding me and she was kind of larger than just a normal size.

As I spoke with her it was sort of filmy and there was an increasing amount of light, but it wasn't bright. I heard a lot of voices around her—she didn't seem to be totally alone, but I couldn't describe those other beings. It was just as if she was out on the leading edge and she could connect, and reach me and touch me and talk to me. I could feel her sort of soothing me, and she was saying, just quietly, ''You must choose, you must choose.'' And then in the middle of my indecisiveness, I got a glimpse of my body. It was like I was with her in this limbo stage, and yet I got a glimpse of my body, and I saw it separating out, like two replicas just floating apart. And I thought, ''Ooh, if I don't get back there immediately, that's going to be it!''

I can remember that whole note of earnestness sort of kept rising. I thought, ''Gee, this is it!'' But then I thought, ''I can't choose, I don't know.'' She just kept quietly surrounding me with that presence of love. ''Choose for the sake of love.'' That was for me the key word in the whole experience. She said, ''You must choose for the sake of love.'' And I knew it wasn't just some *little* love.

Finally, in a sense I chose like that (clicks fingers). There wasn't time for a great discussion about it. There wasn't time for anything much, but it seemed to me that she was impressing on me that I *must* make the choice.

I felt it to be very important and very binding, and I felt like I was claiming my life for the first time. I just felt like I had to do what I knew least about—I felt as if I knew more about dying than I did about living and loving. And I thought, "Well, I must now understand how love is, in the world." I had a sense that I was choosing what I didn't know much about, and what desperately mattered for me to learn about.

Immediately I was back in my body, fully—I mean, it was just like someone pushed me back in there. I remember that it was sort of a yank, and I remember seeing a connection between the up-here and the ceiling, and the down-there, almost like a little slide. Now, I wouldn't say I saw a silver cord, but it seemed like it was a path. And I do remember waking up feeling the agonizing pain. And I started calling out, screaming out, because the nursing staff were probably momentarily gone out, maybe to finish their conference. They were thinking of transferring me to an intensive-care unit, because I looked like I was just slipping away. And it all happened only in that brief moment when they went out, to implement their decision making.

Sister Mary, the head nurse, came back in and saw me in this luminous state, and she immediately recognized, I think, what had happened. I remember her just sort of kneeling down and crying and she said to me later, "This is holy ground." I also had visions of a guide, a young American Indian woman—I could see her with my eyes open, in daytime. I felt as if she was sent to help with the transition, and she seemed very much connected with my grandmother. I didn't know she was American Indian at the time, but I could see her glowing, and so could the nurse. And that was all in the room.

I remember, too, that the pain was my first concern, and when Sister Mary was there it was okay, but as soon as she left it wasn't so okay (laughs). I remember they tried to give me some Narcaine, I think, later that day, which was good. It made me feel a bit more solid, and I think they also decided to stop the injections, and do something else. What in fact happened was that I made a dramatic recovery. They could hardly believe it—my blood pressure came up, and my pulse. So it all kind of came together and I was out of there five days later! It was amazing. They were all nodding their heads and saying, well, maybe they were wrong about septicemia. I felt as if my body was almost filled with a kind of new heaviness, but it was like it was a substantial kind of light. It wasn't a darkness anymore.

I think it's pretty obvious that there were forces of love at work in that experience. I was so curious about death that I might have easily flipped over to saying, "That would be fun to explore." But then I suddenly realized the enormity of it and something else happened that is difficult to put into words—I think I got a sense of my purpose that I'd never seen before. And it wasn't that I didn't have a sense of purpose and direction before, because in fact I had a very strong one, but I think it didn't have much substance until that experience. As a youngster I was extremely prone to writing high-flying statements about why I wanted to be a doctor. But after the experience my purpose wasn't just about little me anymore—it was a purpose that went way beyond me, but included me. I really discovered another level of joy and meaning. There was no coercion whatsoever. "Choose for love"—that's a very enigmatic statement! I remember trying to think, and then realizing that it was beyond mind, and then I just sort of dissolved, my ego dissolved. I was probably a pretty bumptious young doctor at the time. That experience changed all that!

Twelve years later I was raped, but my grandmother was there again, from the beginning. That experience went over about seven hours clock time. It was a dreadful business, just awful. He had two guns and it took me at least ten minutes to actually grasp the fact that it was happening to me. Not much longer, because by then he was marching me across a very dark park and it was obvious he had nothing to rob me of, except life. It was getting toward twilight, and it was winter.

I can remember my grandmother was there first. God bless her, she always seems to be right on the spot when I need her. But I also felt as if my grandfather was there, and my own mother and father, and there was another person there, I guess it was my godmother. But the key people were Grandma and Grandpa, and my mother and father.

And I was talking with this guy all the time. He was very angry and threw me around. Fairly soon, in the cold and the panic, and with the constant reminder of the guns—he was sticking one in my eye and one in my back—my heart was beating like crazy! I don't know how my poor little adrenal glands kept going all that night, but I just felt like I could drop dead of a heart attack. It was so awful. And during that time, I was sort of praying out loud, and talking to the guy—it's just like I was being given the words—and I was seeing my life. It was like a continuous unbroken film of my whole life, of every scene in detail (important incidents and unimportant incidents), a constant stream of consciousness.

I felt like the only action I could take was to prepare to die. I said to him, "Well, I expect I'll be dead tomorrow, so there are a couple of things I'd like to sort of think about or settle." And I was sort of joking with him and saying, "For God's sake, do a good job, don't leave me half-dead. You know I'd either prefer that you really do it, or let me go." It actually caught him in the end, he was interested. I guess not many women in the presence of a murderer would sort of face their death in that way. I think that unnerved him terribly, and my talking about dying all the time sort of made him want to do something else. Anyway, he took a long time to make up his mind and he kept threatening to kill me. Who was I to know that this guy had a terrible record of armed robbery?

That night I felt almost as if I was in my deceased relatives' domain. I felt like I was terribly disembodied—even worse than when I was in the hospital. My brain and everything held together for the duration of that experience, but it might not have for much longer. I ended up having very severe diabetes after that.

The point was that I was so out of my body that there was only a tenuous link between myself and it. I can remember watching him rape me, as if I wasn't quite there. I was going through this whole thing feeling, "Well, I don't want to have my entire soul warped by this experience. I'm just going to withdraw from it." I even experienced a strange kind of exultation that I could cope with all this. I didn't feel I was brave, but I felt as if I was absolutely able to depend on help, *absolutely* able. There was just no question about it—those beings were there, and they were going to help me, whatever way it went. It didn't really matter anymore, because they were there.

I remember thinking that I must not fall asleep, however much that cost me. Between my chattering teeth and my frozen state and my out-of-bodyness, the effort of staying awake was considerable. Because my body was cold (it was like hypothermia), I felt very drowsy, and also it was late and getting later all the time. I wasn't sure I could hang on, and I felt that if I had fallen asleep, he may well have killed me.

During the whole thing I was clear in myself that I really did want to live, but if that was not possible, I felt I'd already lived a good life, I felt that I could have died. I didn't want to die, but if it was going to happen,

I wasn't going to make a big fuss about it. I can remember sort of settling that issue with the rapist near the beginning. I think I even told him that I worked with people who are dying. After it was all over, I don't think I came back to my body for another five months.

Even before the first experience, I never really had a fear of death. As a tiny kid I used to trot around with my mum while she lay out what I'd call "the stiffs." She was a district nurse and I saw death at a young age. Death was not a strange thing at all. It did upset me a little, but not in a conventional sense. I was very curious about it.

And when I was younger, I definitely believed in life after death, although it tended to be a mental sort of thing. As a child my parents spoke openly around the house about life after death and psychic phenomena since they were deeply interested in the works of Rainer Johnson (who was connected with Edgar Cayce and the Society for Psychical Research in London). Yet when I went into medical school I totally forgot all about this stuff! I really forgot it, like it didn't exist. And when I became a licensed doctor, my first eight patients were dead, and I thought, "I wonder what this means." I now wish I had been of more service to them. I wish I hadn't thought to myself, "Oh crumbs, I can't do anything for them!" I could have done something for them—they were dead, but they were still around their bodies.

I suppose I've always been interested in death and dying. Death is as fascinating as birth to me. I didn't particularly choose to specially work in that area, but it has just happened. I guess it did become more of a conscious choice after my daughter died in 1984. And then I felt, "Well, okay." The only way I could recover was to really say, "Yes, I will do this work, but not necessarily full-time." But when I look at my practice, the single most frequent issue to come up is that someone in the family's dying, or they haven't gotten over someone's death. They just keep coming to me. It goes on and on and on, so I see that if it's not a literal, direct problem that someone's dying, it's a psychological transformation of that same kind. So now I admit that's the area in which I have some form of experience.

I would say that from childhood I was deeply concerned about ultimate questions and values and meaning, and religion in the sense of exploring the reality that we live in. But I broke away very quickly from the organized kind of religion before I even left primary school. I was lucky because my family were not strict in that sense—they were Quakers and my dad linked up with a Protestant church and my mother said I ought to study other religions, too. So my parents were both pretty broad-minded intellectually.

I never belonged to any particular denomination, and even now I possibly feel more of an affinity with something like Quakerism or Sufism—something that's universal and embraces all the great religious paths. Without question I think people need the option of different paths.

At the time of my NDE I didn't have much in the way of overtly spiritual practices, because I was consumed by medicine—that was my spiritual life. There wasn't a minute to do anything else. For two or three years on end I would sleep for only two or three hours a night. So after the experience, the actual frailty in my body gave me some time off, and I went to the country and I immersed myself in nature. I did get back to music more, and I also got into a kind of Jungian analysis, all of which I regard as spiritual practices. Later I started yoga, but I didn't start meditation right away because I wasn't well enough. I think I did my meditation in the woods. When I got sick, I can remember actually enjoying the solitude of the sickness. I hated the bodily side of it, but the quietness I enjoyed.

I wanted more solitude. I didn't want to rush back into medicine. I mean, I never bought the whole medical trip ever again. That was finished for me. And that was pretty dramatic, because I was then a very loyalist, dyed-in-the-wood doctor. I always thought I would have a sense of self-worth if I were a doctor, but now I can feel a sense of worth regardless of what I am doing. At the time I was probably pretty insecure unless I was in my doctor role. And that didn't change overnight, but I think I was radically changed. It was time.

My motivation in life was also totally changed, radically changed. Although it was a bit hard at the beginning, it was such a relief to get out of medicine. I found I didn't have my former ambition, to be comfortable and well-off. That was just turned upside down. I don't know whether it had to be, but it was, it happened, and I've been poor ever since.

After the experience I actually went away for an entire year to a really weird guest house where I lived alone, with a mute. So I really withdrew! I wasn't physically very strong, and what I did during that year was to study comparative religion and feel myself hoping I could go to the Jung Institute. I did a lot of yoga and tried to eat better. But mostly I just lived out there alone and it was very cheap and strange and there was always this tiny little thing in my mind: "You will have to make a choice."

I saw almost no one, except the people I had to see—the class and the yoga teacher. The teacher and I had a strong connection but we never talked, I just did the work. I didn't feel like talking, or wasting my energy on anything except getting better. It was a long struggle. I was very exhausted. I had really been secretly wanting to do Jungian studies for a long time, and so I studied and eventually I started at the Jung Institute.

• • •

Today, I love to get out and watch people (laughs), take a ferry ride, play with kids. I can't stand being a passive spectator—I can't stand watching television, it drives me up the wall. I don't even have a television set! I love people, getting together or planning a party, or things like that, seasonal festivities and celebrations. I love simple things. Gardening is one of my big entertainments, if I have the time.

I love going into wilderness areas, taking small groups on wilderness retreats. I really did throw myself into political things as a student (connected with Vietnam and abolition of capital punishment), but now I think I do more politics when I work with people. I have in fact in the last year or two done more peace activists' training than I've ever done before. It's become more introverted. It's really designed for them to know themselves, to know whether the conflict is within themselves. I'm also very involved in the ecology movement, but again it's all based, like the wilderness trips, on getting everyone to be responsible for their own personal ecological situation.

As a child I saw auras and I could tell things. My mother was highly psychic, so it was sort of just taken for granted in the family. It wasn't any big thing. My father was reading books about all these phenomena, and my mum just knew about it. When I went into med school I was almost literally told through dreams that I would lose those gifts for quite some years, so that I could be more in the medical mode, as it were, and in touch with that. I would have to then develop other ways of perception. This was a struggle for me—to use my sensory apparatus instead of my intuition and my psychic awareness.

I feel the last few years I've become a lot more intuitive. I don't know if I'd use the word *psychic*. I don't see auras now much, but I do sometimes. And I do sometimes have extraordinary intuitions about what's going on with people that they just can't believe. But I feel that the psychic power is innate in a lot of us—it might just take different forms.

I feel strongly across the board in therapy, too, that people have the power in themselves. It is not helpful to encourage their getting knowledge from another person, other than that they compare notes. It's important that they do their own thing. I think at times that people only need what I call resources or knowledge. It's important not to talk too much. Sometimes people have to be inspired first, but then when they're up and going, then I leave them to go for themselves.

I don't call myself an analyst so much as a teacher of the ways of the psyche, because I think my job now is to get people to go, study, follow their own interests, not just have me tell them what to do. It's a way of leading people out—true education.

CHAPTER 4

Point of No Return

It had seemed that the boundary between life and death was at the top of the tunnel, where the light was. During the first two experiences I felt sure that ght, I wouldn't come back.
—Olivia

During my own near-death experience[1] I had a similar sensation. I had moved very quickly through a dark tunnel—drawn irresistibly toward a magnificent light. As I approached the light I could see it was like very bright but gentle sunlight. Then I found I could see into the light where there was a beautiful landscape: gently rolling hills, flowers, and grasses rippling in the softest of breezes, and all of this bathed in a golden glow. I very much wanted to continue into this landscape but I was somehow aware that if I went into the light I would not be able to return. So I stopped just short of the light, at the end of the tunnel, and reflected on my situation: I was in the process of giving birth to a baby—I didn't even know whether it was a boy or a girl—and I had another much-loved little boy at home who I knew needed me. The choice was mine: I could go on into the light or go back. I chose to go back for the sake of my babies, but then, I also knew that I was going back for me, too, to have another go at life.

In my case, although there was no apparent reason, I just *knew* that the point of no return was the division between the end of the tunnel and the world of light. Olivia had had a similar feeling until her third NDE when, as she said:

I was surrounded by [the light] but I still came back. I can't explain it.

I am often asked at what point people return, and whether they want to come back. But there is no one answer. It seems that for near-death experiencers generally there is no one "point of return." And as Olivia's experience suggests, the borderline is not necessarily constant even within the experience of one person. Yet in most cases there *is* a definite sense of a boundary—whether visual, auditory or emotional—beyond which experiencers cannot pass. This can take many forms—steps, walls, rivers, bridges, angels, voices and decisions are among the most common.

Hal,[2] a fourteen-year-old at the time of his experience, actually entered the "world of light." But even in that realm there were boundaries beyond which he couldn't pass. He saw a stream, and on the other side of the stream were departed relatives who called to him. But he found he could not cross over. As he said, "It seemed I was in another dimension." He was, however, met on his side of the stream by two deceased school friends who showed him around. When it was finally time for him to go back to his body, his friend took him to a wall. Hal describes what happened:

He took me over to the wall and said, "It's nothing to worry about. You just step out, it's like stepping out of a bubble. And you'll see your body just as soon as you get out."

I went straight through the wall, and I was out of that dimension and back into our own dimension, and I was all on my own. I could see my body and it was blue. I thought I'd better get straight back into it. How I got into it I don't know.

Martine[3] actually found herself moving slowly along a stream, but her worries for her husband and children returned her to her body before she reached the light.

The stream or river is a common boundary reported by Japanese near-death experiencers. And a bridge,[4] as link between the two worlds, is also frequently encountered. On a recent trip to Japan I was fortunate in being able to collect several stories.[5] One concerned a six-year-old child who was in a coma for three days. During her experience she came to the banks of a river. She could see the other side but knew she couldn't get across because it was too wide. On both sides of the river she could see many flowers—dandelions, lotus flowers and many others. As far as she could see there were flowers—she'd never seen such a beautiful sight. Upriver there was a bridge, and she knew if she could reach it she could cross to the other side. She walked and walked and walked but never made it to the bridge. Suddenly she heard someone call her name from behind. She looked but couldn't see anyone. She heard her name called again and then found herself back in her body.

In another Japanese story, a boy of high-school age related that during his experience he found himself on the bank of a river and began to cross a very broad wooden bridge. While still crossing he heard a rhythmic noise approaching from the other side. A man in a rickshaw came close by, stopped and beckoned to the boy. But when he saw the fierce face of the man the boy took fright and ran back the way he had come; and revived from his coma.

Sometimes people find themselves alone at the point of no return, but others find themselves met by a sort of "reception committee" made up of deceased relatives or friends, or even angels. Some choose to return, some are forced to return very much against their will, and others just suddenly find themselves back in their bodies. In the following four stories, Moira found there was a high step to get over before she could enter the "world of light," Patrick came to a wall, Olivia stopped at the end of the tunnel on two occasions, and Anthea was confronted by three angels who gave her a choice.

MOIRA

I first spoke to Moira when she called me after reading an article I had written for a hospice journal. We arranged to meet soon after.

Moira is tall, with white hair and skin of a remarkable translucence. She has a rather deep voice and an exuberant laugh. She literally glows with vitality and looks much younger than her years.

At the time of her NDE she was employed as a teacher of ballroom dancing, but by the time of the interview she was the welfare director of a large charitable organization.

Moira's experience happened when she was twenty-nine and we spoke thirty-four years later, when I went to her pleasantly cool apartment one very hot day early in summer.

I'd been having a lot of pain in my right side, which kept on coming and going and finally got so bad that I was rushed off to the hospital. They diagnosed it as acute appendicitis and operated. But after the operation I just didn't come good—I got worse and worse. On about the fourth day after the operation, I just suddenly let go, I felt tremendously ill. It was as if something inside me was just ebbing away and I was trying to hold on to it. I could feel all my strength going. And I can remember the exact second when I thought, "I can't go on, I've just got to let go, this is the end." Anyway, I let go and then everything was very black. I can remember someone getting a doctor, or people coming around to me, and then it was black, absolute blackness. And it was warm, a warm sort of blackness. I felt as though I was enveloped in warm air.

And then I could see a light right at the very end of what looked like a tunnel. It was a long, long way away, just a very small light. And I knew without doubt that I had to get to that light—I felt a tremendous drawing power—so I started to go toward it. But strangely enough, at the same time there was something holding me back—I felt as if I was wading through water. (You know how when you're wading through water, it's very hard to get your legs through.) But there was no water there, it was as though thick air was trying to hold me back. I was pushing and pushing to get to this light—I knew I had to get there. Eventually it got bigger and bigger and I finally found myself at this light. It was like an enormous lit-up picture window. And there was a very high step to get over before I could get into it.

As I looked through into this tremendous light, I could see there was a glorious garden. It was the most beautiful garden I'd ever seen. There were masses of trees and shrubs and grass and it looked as if it was very well tended, as if hordes of people had looked after it and kept it beautifully. And the whole thing was enveloped in a beautiful golden light. Anyway, as I looked at all this light, I thought how beautiful it was and I knew that I wanted to get into the middle of it. But I felt a profound feeling of disappointment, because no one was there, and I knew that there were going to be a lot of people there waiting for me. (I don't know how I knew that (laughs), it just came into my head.) I was so bitterly disappointed, but at the same time I felt wonderful being there.

I don't know how long I stayed there. I was just lost in this beautiful light and everything. And I had the feeling that the place was teeming with life even though there wasn't a soul to be seen. I felt that everybody must have been hiding behind rocks and trees and (laughs) it was a strange feeling, as if they were all just hiding there. I felt the warmth of them and the love of them, but they wouldn't come out. I kept on struggling to get over this big step while all this thick air (or whatever it was) was pulling me back. I don't know how long I did this, but it went on for quite a while. Then suddenly I made a really enormous effort, because I *had* to get into this garden. Then I heard a voice which said, "You're too early.'' And with that I let go and I went back at a tremendous rate. I felt myself being drawn very swiftly back up the tunnel into the blackness.

And then I awoke and there were all these faces over me and everybody working on me. Apparently I'd just about gone. I didn't find out till a couple of days later, when I was feeling much better, that I'd had a very severe kidney infection. It was nothing to do with my appendix after all. So that was it. After that the feeling stayed with me for such a long while, and even now I can get back into it. At a moment's notice, I can get right back in it and experience it. And I knew from that moment on that there isn't any death, it's just a different state of consciousness. We close our eyes in this room and we wake up in another room, sort of thing.

It all seemed so natural, this is what amazed me. It was just perfectly natural that I be there. The only thing I can consciously remember feeling was the struggle to get there, and the tremendous disappointment that these wonderful beings or people or whoever they were, weren't there. I had the feeling that there would be women there, and men, and children, all sorts of people, just waiting to welcome me and help me, and show me the ropes, as it were (laughs). It felt like a coming home, as though this was a place where I'd been before and, after a long journey, I was coming back to it—almost like the prodigal son returning (laughs).

I now believe I didn't die because it wasn't the right time. I have a very strong feeling that we're here to accomplish certain things. We each have our destiny. I don't mean that our destiny's put on us by someone else. I think that our own higher self works out what we have to do and what's best for us before we get here, and then we do it.

I didn't talk about it at all, not in those days. I mean, thirty years ago you were considered a crank for less than that. I didn't talk about it for many years, because I just knew it was true. I knew it was the truest, most honest thing that had ever happened to me. I didn't for a moment think, "Oh, I'm going around the bend," or "There might have been something gone wrong in my brain." I just knew that that was the truth, and that was the true reality.

I know now that whatever we're living and doing here is only an illusion of reality, it's just something we do until we go back home to this other reality. But at that time I didn't have a very clear philosophy. I knew that there was some sort of God, or supreme being, or some underlying intelligence, but I didn't know what that God was. I'd been indoctrinated by the orthodox churches into the belief that God was sitting up there on a throne, that he had a long white beard (laughs) and would throw out bolts of thunder and lightning every time I did something wrong.

I finally told a couple of my girlfriends about it many years later. They'd been rather worried because they'd had experiences seeing visions and hearing voices. They didn't know what that was all about, and thought perhaps they were going round the bend. Then I told them my experience, and we went on from there.

I hadn't read anything about that sort of thing before my NDE and it wasn't till many years later that I started to encounter books where people had had much the same thing. But after that experience I started investigating. I'd read ordinary books on Christianity and so forth, which always left me very much doubting. I knew there was some underlying God or intelligence, but I felt that the churches had it all wrong (laughs). So I started experimenting. I went to spiritualist groups and I went through all that spiritualism, psychism stage, and gradually moved on from that to other religions—Mormonism, Christian Science, all sorts of things. Gradually I developed my own philosophy: I knew there was a God, but I knew that I wasn't separate. I knew that I didn't need a priest or a minister between me and God, and I knew I was part of God.

I wasn't too sure about what happened at death before my NDE. My upbringing in the Church of England had told me there was a heaven, but I'd also heard about hell and all that sort of thing, which I could never equate with a loving God. I'd thought, "Well, how come if this God's so loving, if I do something bad I'll be cast into hellfire?" In those days I think people believed all that orthodox stuff even more than they do now. I felt like an inner rebel, really. I listened to what everybody said and nodded my head, but inside I thought, "Oh no, no, I can't accept that, that's not right." So I withdrew from the ordinary church.

Now I believe we just move into another stage of consciousness. I believe that this body is the effect of our minds, or our level of consciousness. So at present I have this sort of body, but when I die, I'll go into another, expanded, state of consciousness. I feel that there is no death, we go on for eternity and, depending on our level of consciousness, we might have a spiritual body, or whatever, to use.

I've thought a lot about reincarnation—it's a very good hypothesis—but I don't know whether it's true. I don't know whether I do need to come back to this earth. I think perhaps the nature of things is to progress upward. We might just progress up to another sphere of expression somewhere. I didn't believe in it at all before my experience. I'd thought it was a whole lot of Eastern rubbish (laughs) until I started on my search. Then I started reading Eastern stuff and realized that they knew so much more about it than we do (laughs).

I had a great fear of death before my NDE. I didn't like the idea of death at all. Now I don't suppose I'd welcome it, but I have no fear whatsoever of death. I've also had a few flashes of cosmic consciousness or what

I think is cosmic consciousness, and it's just so much more true and much more real than what we're doing here.

I had no interest in death or dying. I think the questions I was really interested in were: "What's it all about?"; "What are we doing here?"; "What's it for?"; and "Is there a God?" My underlying feeling was that there must be a first cause, or something that initiated this whole thing, but I couldn't accept at all the orthodox explanation.

I've journeyed through so many religions and I've always come up against something that I just couldn't believe. And then I realized, of course, that we don't need any religion, we are a part of God. We are all a part of God, we are immersed in spirit. So although God is not a great big person sort of thing, we are all a part of God. Each of us is like a cell in the body of God, so we have all God's inherent qualities: love, peace, wisdom, etcetera, but we don't recognize it because we have this sense of separation. But once we can get over the sense of separation we'll know who we really are and then we'll be able to start expressing it.

The NDE was for me a really spiritual experience. It showed me that there is rhyme and reason in everything. Before, I could see all the suffering in the world and it seemed like a sick joke. I'd think, "If a loving God brought all this into being, there's no sense to it." But the feeling that I got in that place of light was so wonderful. There was so much warmth and love and bliss—it was a feeling of absolute bliss that vibrated through me—and I thought, "Well, this is the real me, this is my real home, this is where I'm meant to be." So now, whenever things really get me down in life, I can immediately relate back to that and say to myself, "Well, this isn't real, this is just an effect. The real's back there and that's where I'm going when I go home." It's wonderful!

Once that had happened, it was as if I had a solid base to work from. So in the following years I investigated several religions, met some wonderful people and had some lovely experiences, but found that none of them were for me. And then I realized that we don't need religion.

I've had many psychic experiences. Just after [the NDE], I went through a very psychic phase, a clairvoyant phase. I'd moved into a flat with two girlfriends who were interested in spiritualism, so I started going to spiritualist meetings. At first I pooh-poohed the whole thing, but after a while I began to realize that there *was* something there that was inexplicable. I saw visions of angels—well, not angels exactly, but beautiful beings—and I felt as if I was getting direction from them. I didn't say much about this because I thought people'd think I was a bit of a crank.

And I had out-of-body experiences where I went to bed at night and woke up to find myself hovering over the bed, observing my body lying there. And several times I traveled to different places. It was almost as if I took off out of my body at a tremendous speed and went to places like (I know this sounds silly) it was as if I was in Peru. I've never been to Peru in my life, but it was as if I was in Peru and way back, many many years ago. I traveled there, and I saw all these people living in hillside caves and they had quite a good civilization but they just lived in all these caves. They dressed well, they had fires that they cooked their meals on and it wasn't a low-level civilization. They seemed to be pretty knowledgeable sort of people, their caves were very nice and they had a type of furniture and so forth. Whether I traveled back in time or whether it was just a dream I don't know, but I have had several of those sorts of experiences.

I've never done it at will. I have read about people

making up their minds to go someplace, but I have never done that. I have always just fallen into it by accident, it's been the last thing on my mind, and then I've woken up and suddenly found myself there, or it's happened in real life. I know this sounds stupid, but in real life I was walking down the street one day, and I suddenly found myself out of my body, and I was thinking, "How can this be?" I was still walking down the street but I was a couple of paces behind, and I was looking at myself from behind, and I could see every bit of myself. And I thought, "Oh, so that's how she looks" (laughs). It was as if I was looking at somebody else, even though it was myself, because I said "she," I didn't say "so that's how *I* look." I was very aware at that moment that I was just "expressing" in this personality for a brief moment of time and that the "real me" was the me outside.

The same thing happened one day in the city. I had a very bad fall and I felt such a fool. I'd gone into a blouse shop but I hadn't seen there was a step there, and I was reaching up, looking at something on a hanger, and I fell backward, over the step, and pulled the whole rack out with me. I felt like such a fool later when I realized what I'd done. As I fell backward my head went out the door and went bang on the pavement, and I went out with a jolt. I found out later that everybody had rushed over and picked me up, but I felt as if I was lying there for quite a while. And as I was falling I felt myself falling, and time stopped—it just stopped—and I seemed to take years and years to hit. Time just didn't exist anymore, and I was going down and it took ages to hit and when I hit it was a hell of a bump, and then I felt as if I was jolted out of my body. I thought, "Oh, look at her, she's lying there with her clean hair in the dirt" (because I was on the pavement). That was a funny feeling. And as the people rushed to get me up, it was like a jolt—I snapped back into my body—and they sat me on a chair. I was very shaky after that and they were all rushing around, getting me drinks of water and so forth.

I do find that these things happen when I'm out of my usual routine. Both of those experiences happened at a time when I wasn't very happy with life and was wondering, "What's it all about?", and "What am I achieving?" and that sort of thing. But it is quite amazing because I'd never had any psychic experiences at all before my NDE, apart from a few hunches and things like that. There was certainly nothing specific that I can remember.

When I was going through my clairvoyant stage I often found that I got a picture just when I turned a corner. I don't know why, it was almost as if I'd gotten on a new wavelength—I'd turn a corner into my street and then I'd see a picture of a parcel at my front door, and sure enough I'd get there and there it would be. Or I'd turn a corner to visit my girlfriend and I'd say, "Oh yes, Sue is going to get me a lift home tonight," a matter-of-fact sort of thing, with no rhyme or reason for thinking it, and when I got to her place she'd say, "Oh, guess what? Philip's coming around and he's going to drive you home." It became almost a matter-of-fact thing. And the two lasses I was living with, they were always saying, "Oh, what's going to happen? What's going to happen?" So I started telling them all sorts of things that would happen, and sure enough they did.

That was a very, very strong phase I went through with clairvoyance. I suppose it lasted a few years, but I found that it had its traps, too. I loved doing it at first, but then there was the trap of "aren't I clever!" (laughs). At first I thought it was great that I could do something that I couldn't do before, but then the responsibility started to home in on me. I realized that all these people sitting listening would go off and do what

I said, and that was pretty awe-inspiring. I also realized that a lot of people, instead of using their initiative and doing their own thing, started to become dependent on what I was saying. So I withdrew—I didn't like it. I felt it was unethical and too much of a responsibility. I suppose I could have gone on using it, but I put a stop to it. I still get flashes of it, but I don't go out looking for it.

At the time of my experience I believed I was a nothing, that everybody else was far better educated than I. I was a very shy person in those days. Hard to believe now! (laughs). I was very shy, very diffident about my own skills. I had no skills really. I think I was twenty-eight before I was game enough to even have my first dancing lesson, and then within a few years I was teaching it (laughs). I had a good sense of humor, but I could only use it with certain people. I felt as if I was a downtrodden and underneath sort of person in those days, but I guess that was the way I'd been brought up. But since then, absolutely my whole life has changed. It's opened up and I've become more assertive and more aware of who I am. I now realize that I am a perfect being in my own right and I don't have to fear anybody else or anything else. I mean, I'm still the same old Moira making the same mistakes, but I'm much more aware of what's going on. I have much more self-confidence now.

I was never motivated by money—my main motivation before [the NDE] was travel. My father was a sailor, he'd been at sea a good deal of his life and I suppose I was brought up with tales of the sea and tales of traveling. Anyway, I had this tremendous urge inside me to go see the world, never dreaming that I could, because in those days it was impossible for a girl to go to sea. Later on, after I had this experience, in my thirties, I found out that some ships did have stewardesses, but most of them had to go to England and have their first-aid certificate and all that sort of jazz. I didn't have my fare to England, so I just thought, "Well, that's something I'll never do." But as time went on I realized that I *had* to do it. Against all odds, when I was thirty-six I went to sea—I found a job on a Swedish ship.

The way I got that job is very strange. One day I was going down to the station to get the train to work, and once again it was almost as if I was out of my body and as if there was a shift in time. I was on a ship, and the wind and the weather was as rough as it could be. Normally I'm terrified of anything like that, I'm not a brave person at all. Anyway, I was standing on the deck of this ship and the ship was going up and down and the wind was howling, and I was enjoying it, loving it. I felt this great sense of being one with the elements—not a bit scared (laughs). It was the strangest feeling. And then all of a sudden I was back in my body and walking off down to the station. Suddenly I heard a voice in my right ear say, "Learn Swedish." It was so loud that I looked round into a front garden on my right to see if there was anybody there, but there wasn't. And I got this "Learn Swedish" pounding in my ear all day. "Learn Swedish, learn Swedish. You must learn Swedish," and it drove me silly all day long. So I made some inquiries, and found they didn't teach Swedish at the university then and nobody knew Swedish in those days. I tried everything I could think of. I never was able to learn it, but soon after I got a job on a Swedish ship.

The way that happened was strange, too. I'd kept on going into this Swedish Shipping Line office, and they kept on saying, "Oh, run away, run away." So next I went round to the Swedish Consulate and I said, "Look, I'm desperate to get a job." And he said, "Well, I've got a waiting list this long," and showed me this great list. He said, "You will never get a job on a Swedish ship, just go away and forget about it. Occasionally we put someone on down here if a Swedish girl gets sick, but you'd have to be terribly lucky.'' So off I went toward home.

I was going down the street toward the station and a voice said to me, in my ear once again, ''Go back! Go back to the office that you've just come from.'' So I stood in the middle of the road and I thought, ''Now, will I go back?'' And I thought, ''I can't, he's just told me to go away and not come back. How can I go back?'' In those days we wore hats and gloves and all that, so I thought, ''Well, the only thing I can do is go back and ask if I'd left my gloves behind.'' I had to tell a lie to get an excuse for going back. And I thought, ''This is mad! I'll go back down to the station.'' I went a few steps, then I heard the voice again: ''Go back! Go back!'' so I went back. As I walked in the door this man was just putting the phone down, and he looked at me with eyes like saucers and he said, ''Miss Pollard, I'm just absolutely overwhelmed, what are you doing here?'' I said, ''I've lost my gloves. Did I leave them here?'' looking around, pretending to look for my gloves (laughs). He said, ''The mess boy's just taken sick—can you go down?'' I said I'd go down immediately. So I walked out the door, and would you believe, there was a taxi outside the door. I jumped in the taxi and we drove down to the docks and I got the job. That's how it turned out. I had three days to sell all my furniture and go to sea. And I did it!

Everyone said, ''You're mad! You'll be back! You get sick on anything that moves.'' But when I got on that ship and I felt the movement, I knew I'd been there before and I knew this was meant to be. I had six wonderful years, and that was only by listening to the voice in my ear. If I hadn't listened to that I would have missed out.

I love nature, particularly trees. I have a great affinity with trees because my grandest, most wonderful experience was with trees. I'm aware that every plant, every tree, everything has got a consciousness of its own, and that we are one with it, if we only knew. And we can communicate, in a way, with them. I mean, we're self-knowing, the tree isn't self-knowing, but we are one.

The experience with the trees happened when I was in my forties. On the basis of what I already knew from my NDE, it gave me such strength. It confirmed that I'm very much more than this physical person sitting here.

At that time I'd been very ill and going through a lot of pain. At one stage I started to wonder whether I'd been putting myself on all these years—perhaps there wasn't a God. I was agonizing, "God, are you really there?" This day I managed to drag myself off my bed to do some washing. At the back of where I lived then we had two beautiful gum trees—white trunks, really enormous—and over the years I'd built up a sort of relationship with them. I felt the presence of them whenever I went past, and as I went past this day I looked at one of them and quite spontaneously said, "Oh, I do love you!" And that was the first time in my life that I'd ever said "I do love you" to anybody or anything without thinking of getting something back. This was a pure outpouring of love. It really surprised me.

At that instant, as I looked at the tree, it was as if I had X-ray vision—I could see inside the tree—and I could see all these cells working away like mad. As I looked at them I became a cell, and there I was and I had a consciousness. I couldn't think or reason, but I had a feeling of joy that I was there doing something to help the universe go round. I was helping bring up all this sap or whatever it was, up into me to pass on to the next one, to the next one to the next one, to the top of the tree. And there was a feeling of joyous participation in something that just went on and on. It was a great feeling, but then suddenly I found myself back in my body.

I was so stunned that I started pegging the washing on the line. Then the same thing happened again—I suddenly had this X-ray vision—I could see through all the trees, through everything, and I could see that absolutely everything in the universe was interconnected, and interdependent. There was nothing separate, not a thing. Then I saw that even the air between things was just teeming with organisms, and they were all interconnected and all for a purpose. They were all doing things. They were going into me and coming out, going into the earth and coming out, going into the trees and coming out. I could see that absolutely everything was interconnected. And I thought, "So that's how it works!"

I completely lost consciousness of myself—I don't know how long it lasted—I could see through all the trees, all the buildings, and I could see to infinity. Then the next thing I knew, I was out in space somewhere, and I knew that the same power that was holding all the planets and everything in space was the same power that was in me. And it's a stupid sort of thing to say, but I didn't see God—I felt I *was* God! I suddenly felt that I knew everything, that I was everything (laughs). You see words don't explain it. I knew I knew everything, I knew there was an absolute reason for being, and I knew that the universe was all one—almost as if the universe was me and I was the universe.

I don't know how long that lasted, but when it finished I came back, and it was as if I was numb. I couldn't think, I just went on putting clothes on the line, then I walked into the laundry and put the basket down. I walked up around the house, and into the kitchen. And as I walked out of the sunlight I had the most amazing feeling of waves and waves and waves of ecstasy going through me, vibrating all through me to the tips of my fingers. It was bliss! I couldn't stand up, so I fell into a chair, and I just sat there like that for ages. And I kept thinking, "Why did this happen to me? Why was I shown this?"

Eventually it wore off, but that was the greatest thing that ever happened to me, and I've had a few flashes of it since. I would like to say that it really changed my life, that I became absolutely perfect, pure and holy, but I didn't. I just went on making the same old mistakes, doing the same old things, but underneath there was a knowingness, an absolute knowingness that it wouldn't matter who threatened me or what went on in the world, I would always know that I am a part of God and that there is no death. It was absolutely wonderful.

My lifestyle today has meaning—it didn't have meaning before. I think I used to feel that I was just drifting along on a current of life, and I didn't know where I was going or what I was doing. But after that experience I knew there was deep meaning to everything. Everything is connected. Everything has meaning, and everything is a step along the way.

PATRICK

On one of my interviewing trips to the north, I drove to a small village on a quiet, wide expanse of water just south of Brisbane. There were dinghies pulled up onto the sand and waterbirds wading in the shallows. A couple of streets back from the water I located Patrick's house—typical of houses in that part of the country, it was built high off the ground to take advantage of the sea breezes. It was set in a magnificent garden of tropical vegetation. Everywhere there were brightly colored birds darting from tree to tree and calling so loudly that at times their calls are all that can be heard on the tape recording of the interview. After a welcoming cool drink, Patrick and I sat on the wide veranda to talk. His wife and my husband sat close by, listening.

Patrick is a big man—tall, with faded red hair and fair skin, very friendly and obviously enjoying his retirement. At the time of his near-death experience he was twenty-three years old and serving in the British army. We spoke together forty-eight years later.

I've always been a sensitive sort of fellow, so the war, the atrocities and the senseless killing really got to me. I think that, combined with the harsh living, gave me arthritic fever, and I had a nervous breakdown at the same time. So when I came home on leave I didn't go back. They rushed me to the hospital unconscious. The first thing I knew, I was being wheeled down the corridor to the elevator, and I couldn't move a muscle, not even blink an eye. I heard the nurse there say, "This one is rheumatic fever, and he's not expected to live the night." So, I thought to myself, "Thanks very much!" (laughs), but I wasn't scared. I was just disappointed to think that there I was, only twenty-three, and I'd soon be gone. After that I didn't know anymore. (Apparently they were changing my pajamas six times a night, and I went down to about six stone [about eighty-five pounds].) I was near death obviously, because they told my parents to come in and see me. The first I knew of this was when I woke up and saw that they were standing at the foot of the bed, crying. I had about a two weeks' growth of beard and I'd confounded them by coming round.

But during that time I went through a tunnel. It seemed as though I was traveling very fast and there was a vague swooshing noise. I know it's an old hack story, but I went through this tunnel, and it wasn't a continuous straight tunnel, it was a sort of winding affair, and I saw a light at the end and I came to see a wall. I imagined it was a brick wall, but I couldn't tell you exactly. But people were going straight through it to the other side. They were just white shapeless forms, but I knew they were people. I hadn't seen anybody till I got there, then they seemed to be passing me when I stopped. You know they'd *sshhooo* straight through the wall. While I was stopped there a voice said to me, "Well, if you go through the wall, you don't get back. If you go through like those people, you've got to stay there, you can't get back. Make up your mind—if you go through, you stay."

I could see a golden light and I could see there was a city there, brightly enveloped in this golden atmosphere. I couldn't say there were buildings there, yet I knew there were buildings, if you know what I mean. There was no shadow, not like the sun casting a shadow here. The light was all around, it was all-enveloping, there was no shadow at all. It was so perfect and I was in such perfect peace. I knew nobody there. I was completely on my own except for this wonderful presence. The voice was softly spoken and yet I felt it could reach into the universe. There was no question of shouting, but the control was there, if you know what I mean. It was an all-embracing thing—this voice didn't seem to belong to anybody in particular, but the light, I suppose, is part of it. And there was no time, time had gone. Eternity was there, there was no concept of time either backward or forward. I could encompass the whole lot, and I could encompass the whole universe. This understanding was the most amazing part.

Then the voice said to me, "It's not your time yet. You should really go back, but you can make up your own mind—it's your choice." So I thought of my father and mother, and then I said, "Well, I'm only twenty-three, I've got a lot to do, so I'd prefer to go back." He said, "The choice is yours." And that was the end of it, really.

Although my first thought was for my father and mother, I really felt I had to come back to do more for my own development—I knew I hadn't completed what I'd been sent here to do. Nevertheless, when I first found I was back, I was disappointed. But then I was glad that I'd been given a second chance, and I knew that I'd be stronger for having had the experience. From that time on I changed my whole life.

Before [the NDE] I'd never thought much about death, although I'd actually seen many dead relatives. (In England people were laid out for a few days before they were buried.) But then during the war, I was horrified by what I saw. There was a lot of meaningless death—it was a terrible waste of life. But after the experience, I had no fear of death at all, none at all. Now I'd be glad of it, really—I'd say, "Well, take me home!" You know, no bother! (laughs).

I soon realized, of course, that I'd be taken for some sort of crank if I tried to talk about it. I did try and venture it from time to time, but it was pooh-poohed in many ways. I thought, "Until I meet a brother in this experience, I can't talk about it." I think when you have these experiences, you don't actually fit into the mold of everybody's thinking anymore. You're sort of released from the common mind, if you like. But if you meet someone who's had one of these experiences, you have a direct brother/sister approach immediately, which you sometimes haven't got with blood relationships. My brother was very dear to me, but in this sort of thing we were poles apart. I wasn't really able to talk to my family about it at all.

I tried to find something to read about it. Quite soon after [the NDE] I picked up the Bible (my father thought I was mad) and I found that although I couldn't believe in Jesus Christ, I did believe in a creator.

I think of the NDE as a spiritual experience—not

religious, because religion to me is man-made. I never was very religious, although I've had experience of many religions. I went to church with my grandmother in a Salvationist church, I went to a Church of England school and I married a Catholic. I have a very diverse religious background, but I can't say that I found any of it very convincing. Today I consider myself to be spiritual. I believe now that one can tap in to the universal experience—the world is a complete entity, a living thing, and we're a part of it. And I think it's important not to divorce ourselves from that.

I always knew that psychic phenomena happened because my mother was part Romany Gypsy—third generation—and she was very psychic. I knew she was, because I was not a great letter writer, and when I joined the army I didn't write home for six months. That was very callous of me. And one day I suddenly got leave unexpectedly and I caught a lift home on the back of a truck. I got home late at night, about ten o'clock, and the house was locked and in darkness. So I threw a pebble up at the window and my mother put her head out: "Oh, it's you, Patrick. Your dinner's in the oven." I thought, "Well, how did you know that?" That was the first thing.

Later on, I was home on leave and the dog was sitting outside the gate. He sat outside this gate for the first day and he wouldn't go away and he wouldn't drink and he wouldn't eat. So my mother said, "Something's happened to Eric" (my brother who was in Africa at the time). And I said, "How would you know?" And she said, "I just know." Anyway, the dog sat there for three days, and didn't eat or drink. After three days the dog came inside and went about normally, and she said, "Eric's either dead or he's got well." Three days later we had a telegram from Cairo saying that he'd been in a hospital near-death, and he was now on the mending list. My mother knew that.

Another case, of course, was when my youngest boy was born. He was in the hospital seriously ill, and he had an operation and was not expected to live. I knelt down in the lounge room and prayed till sweat was on my brow, then the whole thing was lifted from me—I got up suddenly from the floor and danced around the living room. Later on, the next day, we received a call saying that he was going to be all right, and I said, "I know that." And I was seventeen miles away.

I know from my own experience that these things happen. I also realize that whatever happens, it is for the better. I'm not worried by anything, even things that seem to go against me, because I know it's all in the plan and it's for my own good. I remember once, when I was a young boy, I hammered on the window and said, "Mum, let me go out to play" and she said, "No, it's going to rain," and my whole world seemed to break up because my mates were out there and I was indoors and I thought she was very cruel. But all of a sudden it poured with rain and everybody got drenched, and I realized it was for my own good. I think I've carried that example through my life with me, because I really know that whatever happens, it's for my own good. I definitely have a sense of being guided and looked after.

Since the experience I've really grown in self-confidence and self-esteem. I couldn't enter a room with people at one stage, and I'd walk on the other side of the road rather than have to talk to someone. But now I'm the first one to speak if I'm in a line. I always used to admire my grandfather—he'd go up and talk to anyone at a bus stop. I didn't dare, I had no self-confidence at all. But after [the NDE] I knew there was somebody or something looking after and directing me.

I have a sense of purpose now in life, but I'm not at

all motivated by material wealth. In fact, since that time I've always thought that great wealth would destroy me, and therefore I haven't gone in for lotteries or that sort of thing. I have a sense of foreboding that I'm going to win a big prize, and I know it would destroy me. I think I'm supplied with our needs but not our wants—it's a different thing. A person said to me the other day that he regards me as a poor relation. And I said, "Well, what is rich and what is poor?" A person with plenty of money and plenty of assets—a Mercedes and a boat—they may be materially happy but they might be very poor in spirit.

I'm much more interested in the spiritual side of life. I really appreciate nature. It's beautiful! It's wonderful! Even the smallest bug, the way it's painted, the way it moves—it's incredible! I've always liked to walk in the woods and see the marvels of creation. There's no doubt the creator's a mathematician and he's an artist. The natural world is very important to me.

Obviously, the most significant change since [the NDE] for me is that death now has no fear associated with it. That to me is clear. I've been born again, if you like. Death has got no hold over me at all. And (laughs) I think my wife will attest that I've gradually become more serene over the years. I sometimes blow up, but I've got the wrong color hair to be serene all the time (laughs).

Olivia

I first heard about Olivia through one of her friends who attended a talk I gave at a meeting of the Australian Institute for Parapsychological Research. Soon after we made contact I went to her home, which was situated on a noisy main road in an outlying western suburb of

Sydney. Once through the front door, however, there was a noticeable atmosphere of peace.

Olivia is calm, softly spoken and sensitive, yet one has the impression that she is extremely astute and capable of handling just about anything that might arise. She is of slight build with dark, wavy hair worn back from her face. She has a gentle smile and an aura of loving warmth about her.

Olivia has had three near-death experiences: the first, aged twenty-five, during the birth of her first child; the second, aged forty-two, during a hysterectomy; and the third, aged forty-nine, during a long illness. We spoke a year after her third experience, when she was fifty years old. At the time of her first NDE she described herself as a housewife, but by the time of the others, she was working as a hypnotherapist and psychic.

The first one happened just after the birth of my first child, when I hemorrhaged very badly three times. My husband was called back to the hospital for the third time and I was aware that I was lying on the table and the doctors and nurses were working on me. I felt a floating experience and I could see my own hand lying on the table. I had tubes in the left hand and the doctor was working on the right hand, and he kept turning it over to put a needle in the back of the hand and it kept flopping back again. I could see this—I was just above my body. And it didn't worry me particularly. I thought, "That's my hand, I can make it stay still." This happened two or three times, but I couldn't make that hand stay still, so I knew that I was well and truly out-of-body.

And then I heard the sister say, "She's going, doctor," and from that point on, I went. I went into something that appeared to be like a tunnel, and I was moving very fast. There was a roaring noise like a very high wind, yet I wasn't really afraid. I was uncertain, but I wasn't really afraid. There was light at the end of the tunnel and it was glowing. It was very welcoming and warm, and I wanted to get there. I was more concerned about getting there than staying where I was. I almost reached the light, but then I stopped. I looked back and it was as though I was very, very high above the hospital. It was as though someone had taken the roof off a doll's house—I could see all the little rooms. I could see my husband in an anteroom off the operating room, with his head in his hands, and I could see my baby in a crib with various wires and things attached to her—she wasn't well either. I could see myself lying on the table, and I could see the people around me.

Then I heard a voice saying very clearly, "What do you want to do?" I was given the choice, but I knew I had to go back. I knew I'd only been asked the question because I had to go back, I was needed. And I said, "I have to go back." And the voice said, "Yes." And I went back down and came back into myself again. It was a faster descent than it was ascent. I seemed to go back very, very quickly—it was like being drawn down a vacuum—and the first thing I remember was a sister saying, "I've got a pulse."

After I came back to myself I was very aware that this was the hard end, and that the other end was very beautiful. It was a very, very spiritual experience, a very warm and compelling experience.

The second one happened after a hysterectomy operation. I'd been six and a half hours in surgery, and again there were complications and again I hemorrhaged. It was virtually the same thing, except that at that particular time I was going through a rather rough patch and I really didn't want to come back. I went through the tunnel again, and there was glowing light at the end of the tunnel. It was very warm and it seemed very soft. I don't know why I felt the softness, but there seemed to be a lot more softness there. But the question wasn't put to me that time. What I did hear that time was a directive that I had to go back, that it wasn't my time. It had to be put that way because I'd made a conscious decision in my mind that I wanted to stay there. But I had to go back and I went back into my body very quickly.

Getting back into the body was strange. I know how it happens when I trance, but this was different. With trancing, there's a feeling of something going in as you're going out, sort of like the clutch and the accelerator on a car. It's important to get that balance, and then it's very comfortable. But this was entirely different, because it was beyond my control and very fast. The first time it was actually a bit of a shock, but the second time I accepted it because it seemed familiar.

When I came back I thought, "Oh, I'm here again." It was quite a letdown, because it was so comfortable and warm up there and I knew I had problems to contend with when I came back. On a personal level, it was the beginning of the breakup of my first marriage. So again, it was a very emotional experience. But that second time I was told quite clearly it wasn't my time and that I wasn't going to be allowed to stay there. I had to go back. I knew there was no possibility of arguing or bargaining (laughs). I was quite happy to be out of the physical world at that stage—it was a very difficult period in my life and I think it would have been a lovely form of escape if I'd been able to go. But I did go back, and the feeling when I got back was that it was quite a letdown.

The third one was a bit different. It happened last year—I'd had a very bad virus that'd gone on for months and months and months and months. I normally don't take antibiotics, and even though I did take them at that time, it still got worse and worse. It had actually developed into a form of meningitis. I was off for about seven or eight months, and I got very, very thin, and I really thought there was something drastically wrong.

This particular night I had a meditation group meeting. I was going to call it off because I was feeling extremely ill, but I didn't. Several people commented on the fact that I wasn't looking well. This was a group of people who were developing their psychic abilities. I am a trance medium, but at that stage I was withholding going into deep trance because I was helping the others. There was a group of maybe ten or twelve people in the room, and as we went into meditation I was aware that I was going in very deeply. It was that same pulling feeling, of being pulled up, through something, and I thought, "I can't do this in the group," but it didn't make any difference, I still went. It was the same feeling of being pulled up through a tunnel, and there was a light at the top glowing. This time I did go through into it. (Just before I went into that tunnel, or into the light, I remember thinking, "I'm not breathing," but then I went and I had no control over it.)

I was surrounded by the light that time, and—it sounds poetic but it's exactly as I saw it—there was a circle of hands coming through the light. I was in the middle of them and they were all held out toward me. They were individual hands and the palms were up, very gently, and they were all glowing. It was the most incredible feeling, it really was. I still can't talk about it even now without getting emotional, because there was an enormous amount of love there. It was pure love and pure light. That's the only way I can describe it.

I was in the middle and the hands were all held out toward me. There was nothing spoken, yet there was a communication in my mind. I didn't hear the words in a voice as I had before, but the words were there in my mind. I asked if I was dying and the answer I got back was, "No, it isn't time yet." I was told that this would be a turning point, and from here on I would recover, I'd get better. I asked if I could stay there because it was beautiful, it was just so beautiful, but the answer was that it wasn't time, that I had to go back. So I came back. I think I must have received a lot of healing that night, because after that experience I did start to get better.

Up till then it'd seemed that the boundary between life and death was at the top of the tunnel, where the light was. During the first two experiences I felt sure that if I'd gone into that light, I wouldn't have come back. Yet the third time, I was surrounded by it but I still came back. I can't explain it.

When I revived, one of the group who was more experienced than the others said he thought I'd died. He said, "You stopped breathing." He didn't touch me, but he was very, very concerned. He said, "Your face just went blank for so long, and I thought you'd died." So that was to me a very definite near-death experience, even though it wasn't clinically documented like the others. I wasn't in a hospital, but I'd been through it twice before, and I recognized it only too well.

After the first experience, I talked about it with my husband. I guess he was just very, very relieved that the baby and I were both alive—he wasn't aware of anything on a psychic level. I also tried to talk about it with the sister who was in the operating room with me. She said it was something that a lot of people had experienced. She couldn't explain it, but she said she had no doubt that it'd happened, because so many people had spoken to her about it. I also talked about it when I was studying for a degree in psychology, but it was very much a no-no to bring the psychic into psychology in the late seventies. It was very much swept under the carpet—they really didn't want to know about it, it made them very uncomfortable. That's why eventually I discontinued studying. It seemed I had to choose one or the other.

After the second experience, my life changed course dramatically. It took five years, but it was quite a dramatic transition. I changed the country I lived in, I broke up a twenty-eight-year marriage, and I walked away from all the material possessions that I had at that particular time. You don't go through a near-death experience without getting things into perspective. It really altered my life. I've come through some quite amazing things and I guess, since that first experience, I've always felt that there's a reason for me being in this life, but I'm not very clear on what it is.

I suppose I'd always believed in life after death, although I did fear it. At the time of my first experience, I was already aware of reincarnation, but I didn't have the firm belief or the understanding of it that I have now. At that stage I was mostly occupied in getting a home together and attending to all the physical things in life. Today, though, I have no fear of death at all—it's not that I particularly want to die, it's just that I don't have any fear of it. I certainly would never take my own life—suicide has always been a very strong no-no to me. Unless someone's dying of a very painful disease (in which case I think they have every right to decide whether they end it quickly), I don't think suicide is a good idea.

Before my NDEs I was never interested in death at all, but today I deal a lot with people who are getting over grief. I find that by sharing my experiences with them, I can make them feel a whole lot better, so I do use them in that way.

I think of [the NDE] as a spiritual experience, but not a religious one. I was brought up in the Jewish faith, until my father died when I was seven. After that I was brought up in my mother's faith, which was Presbyterian. So I had a very solid religious background, which I walked away from at fourteen or fifteen. I'd decided I was going to wave the banner and become an atheist. It didn't last very long before I started calling myself an agnostic. Then I gradually found that I, in fact, had a very strong *spiritual* belief—not a religious one—it's very different.

I still don't identify with any religion. I think we all have a core of spirituality within us and it doesn't really matter what you call it. Not since childhood have I adhered to any particular religious sect or church or belief. I've always had this concept of religion being within, not outside, that's why I'm not a church person. I think I've always prayed, but now I also meditate.

I always believed in psychic experiences, because I had some when I was fourteen or fifteen that were quite convincing. These have increased dramatically over the years, and now I experience a vast range of them. I am clairvoyant, and I've always had flashes of precognition, right from being very little. It's increased enormously through the years. I've had a lot of supernatural rescues too, thank God! (laughs). They've increased enormously over the last fifteen years, they really have, and particularly so over the last five years, it's quite incredible. Since the second NDE they've increased enormously. I don't get help all the time, but the help that has come through has been in the nature of large miracles at times. I'm almost scared to talk about it in case it goes away, because it's an incredible thing. For instance, if I've fixed my mind on something, and I'm really sure that this is what I need (and I mean need, not want), even if it seems almost an absolute impossibility, if I reach out and ask, I can feel wheels turning, and in a matter of time it comes to me. It may take a year, or eighteen months—it may even take two years—but it never takes any longer than that. It's incredible. I think that capability is probably there within us all—it just takes half your life to learn how to use it!

I feel there is an inner source of wisdom—it's there in everybody, it's not specifically mine. It's just a matter of getting in touch with it, and accepting it, and having faith in it. Of course, for all of us there can come a time, a personal crisis, when it doesn't seem to be there and this is when you know you really are left to find a solution for yourself. You're given a lot of help, a lot of support and a lot of comfort sometimes, but you're not given the answer because it's something you have to work out yourself, but you know that that inner peace, that inner core is still there.

I very much have a sense of being guided—even more so in the last ten years. When I broke up my first marriage, I had this very strong sense that I was being guided, and that I was doing what I had to do. I was like a child being led along a path—that was the feeling I had and I've had it ever since. Of course we *are* children, spiritually we really are. That's the feeling I have—no matter how wise we think we are, we are still children and we are still being led very gently along a path that will lead to light.

I've always been given a lot of information through my dreams and that's increased enormously in the last five years. It's always been there, but earlier in life it only happened on odd occasions. I've had many precognitive dreams, and they've come true quite dramatically at times. But over the last five years or so I've been so busy working with a lot of different people that I guess at night in dream form is when I can really get answers through. I've got to this stage where if I really have questions about something, I can go to bed, send the question out and ask for the answer to come to me during the night, and then go to sleep. And it will cut through a dream I'm having, and it will be symbolic or realistic, but the answer is there for me. And I wake up and I know that that's the answer. The answers are always nitty-gritty truths—they're not always what we want to hear, but they are always right.

I've done a bit of astral traveling, too. Some years ago we sold a house in New Zealand that I'd loved very much, and when we came over here I would go into meditation and go into trance and then find myself back at that house again. I was able to tell my family that the new owners'd chopped down certain trees, and painted the house in what I thought was a horrible color, they'd put in a concrete path and made certain other alterations. I was really annoyed that they'd chopped those trees down, but my husband at the time ridiculed me and said, "You couldn't possibly know that." Two years later I went over there and the people *had* painted the house and the trees *had* been chopped down and the path *had* been put in, so I was seeing it as it was.

At first it was involuntary. The first time I found myself walking up the long winding drive, I thought, "What am I doing here?" And I remember thinking, "Am I really here?" I kicked at the gravel and it seemed so real, but I realized afterward what had happened. After that I tried to see if I could get there again. I've also tried it more recently with my daughter who is in Cairns. I've achieved partial success, but I've never ever been able to do it as well as I did with that house. It was just that it was such a happy place, I had a strong feeling there.

I have had a lot of contact with spirits and guides—both other people's and my own. I didn't have this ability at all before the first NDE. I suppose I was always aware of something being there, but I didn't know whether I feared it or respected it. But now I have sources that I work with very extensively, and I have a lot of faith in them.

I see auras but I don't really have healing powers—

I feel that I'm not a healer, not in a physical sense, although I think I can help people psychologically and spiritually. And that's what I aim to do. Although oddly enough, when I am working with someone, if I run my hand along their body when they're in a state of relaxation, I can feel the sore spots. I'll say to them after, "Have you got a sore stomach or a bad shoulder?" (or whatever) and the answer is always yes. But I don't really know where to go from there.

I didn't do any of this before the first experience. The clairvoyance came through very strongly after that, after my daughter was born. I grew up reading palms, because my grandma had taught me, but I don't think I was really doing anything then, apart from just looking at people's hands. It was after the first experience when my daughter was about a year old that I got one or two very strong directives. I was being told that I should develop more, that I should look for answers. I kept thinking that it was all my imagination, so I asked for proof that it wasn't just my imagination. The proof came through very clearly in a very matter-of-fact way.

After that I became very interested in meditation, and I started developing and exploring that. I was soon made aware that there were many levels of meditation, and I found I could go in deeper and deeper, and from that developed the trance work. But the speaking in trance and the total acceptance of it really only came after the second near-death experience. I also do automatic writing. I get a lot through that way and I find it a lot less exhausting than the trance work. In all honesty, I prefer to use automatic writing—I find it just as good—but in a group, people are often more impressed by something that's invisible. I don't do too much of it now because it is exhausting, but if people are going to give it more credence, I use it. Everything that comes through, whether it's in writing or a speech, makes an awful lot of sense.

One night some years ago, I was very dramatically given a precognitive vision. I have had this sort of thing happen several times, but this was the most dramatic. I was at a circle meeting, and the whole evening, every time I tried to go into meditation, all I could get was a plane floundering through white, which was snow. And right at the end of the evening, I went very deeply in and it was all white. For a moment I saw the tail of a plane with the symbol for Air New Zealand. And then I saw rows of people each with a black box over their head—there were hundreds of people killed. And for a moment—this wasn't very pleasant, this is where I broke off from it, I think I was depressing everybody else there—for a moment there was the wreckage of the plane, the jagged metal and what have you. And a hand came up, reached up just above his face, and it was a man's hand with a ring with a black stone, like a peace ring, and as it reached up it just fell down again and there was blood trickling down between his fingers. This wasn't very pleasant, and it was a little bit too much for me at that time, and I wasn't really happy with it, so I broke off. Actually I broke the circle, because all of that night, every time I closed my eyes, the whole thing came rushing back in again. The woman who ran the circle felt sure I was picking up something that was going to happen. She actually called Air New Zealand to tell them and they absolutely pooh-poohed it. In the morning my husband phoned me and said, "I've just heard the news," and the details fitted in exactly. There have been a lot more since then, but they're not pleasant, because you can't do anything.

There was another occasion after the second NDE. I asked at the time why I had to experience it, because it was very heavy and very unpleasant. I had a broken arm and I was driving along this sort of country road with this one arm in plaster. It was the morning that an almost brand-new plane had crashed and killed the pilot. I kept getting the smell of burning, and it was worrying me enormously. I couldn't pull over because it was a very narrow road. It was like rubber burning, and I kept getting smoke and yet I couldn't see the smoke, so I knew the smoke was psychic. I just hoped and prayed that the burning was, too, because I couldn't stop and I couldn't do anything, and I could feel myself slipping away. Anyway I managed to retain enough consciousness to steer the car. (I was obviously picking up on that pilot, because that was the very time that he nose-dived.) The engine noise got louder and louder and louder until it was a screaming of the plane, in a dive, and the smoke was billowing all around me. I could still see the road and I was still driving the car, but I had this dreadful, horrible feeling that I was going to be killed. I felt I was heading for the ground, and there was nothing I could do, and the tension built up and up and up, and the screaming was getting louder and louder, and then there was just an almighty smash. It left me absolutely shaken—I was covered in perspiration, my heart was pounding, but I was still managing to keep the car on the road.

When I got home my eldest daughter was there. I walked in and I was shaking, I really was. She said, "Are you all right, Mum?" And I said no. She was going through a stage where she thought what I was doing was just too silly for words (which didn't last very long), but she made me a cup of coffee, and I gradually recovered and told her what had happened. Then my husband called and I told him about it, and I called a psychic friend and told her about it. She phoned me later in the morning and said, "What you experienced this morning actually happened." She'd heard it on the news. So I actually picked that up as it was happening. And I can't see what good it could possibly do except put me through such a terrible experience, but those things do happen.

• • •

My whole attitude to myself has changed enormously since the near-death experiences. My self-esteem and sense of self-worth have grown enormously. I guess I'm still fairly reserved, but I do now reach out and talk to people. I'd always had lovely homes, and they were very important to me. The material things in life were very important to me up until the first experience. After the second one, within five years, I literally walked away from everything, and left everything behind. The funny thing was that most of it came back to me later anyway, but it didn't matter. It was a wrench on the physical level, but another part of me knew it didn't matter. Even things that had been given to me, that had sentimental value, they weren't important. Other things were far more important.

My highest priority in life today is spirituality, beyond a doubt, way and above anything else. My children are now grown up, and so the way is clear for me to concentrate on what I'm doing. My second husband is very accepting, and that's an enormous help. I now have an awareness of the size and the extent of the spiritual being in all of us, whereas before, my life was very self-centered. Today the work I'm doing is what I live for.

ANTHEA

By the time I began my project I had already known Anthea for about five years. Since I knew she was working as a hypnotherapist and psychic healer, I thought she might have come across people who had had near-death experiences, so she was one of the first people I called. She laughed when I asked her: ''Oh, Cherie, I've had one of those! You can interview me if you like.'' Neither of us knew until that time that the other had had an NDE. We were both amused to think that we had kept that part of our lives a secret. As we talked the following week I was astonished to hear her story.

Anthea is a small woman, with expressive eyes and a smiling face. She has short, dark, curly hair and fair skin, with rosy cheeks. At the time of her NDE she was thirty-two years old and working as a school librarian. We spoke eleven years later.

I was in the hospital at the time and it was about a day after I'd had a hysterectomy. I'd picked up an infection and was pretty sick.

I was aware of myself being asleep, then suddenly I found myself going through a tunnel. At the end of the tunnel I met three angels and I knew they were angels because they had wings and were dressed in white and, this may sound ridiculous—one of them was seventy feet tall, and I knew she was because she told me so. I felt, the whole time I was journeying, that my physical body was not with me, and I was aware of the smallness of my being. I felt very humble. I felt very small, very insignificant, yet I felt very loved at the same time. I was aware of myself as being like a tiny little pinprick, especially when I looked up and saw this towering huge angel in front of me. The other two were about the size of an average human being. The one who was seventy feet tall was the main angel, and she spoke to me. Her voice was very clear and very warm, with a very loving tone. And she said, "You are with us on the other side. Now you have a choice—you can come with us and we will take you further, or you can go back to where you were. It's up to you."

I felt really warm and very loved. I felt like I really wanted to be there—it wasn't frightening, just very loving. I really wanted to go with them, because it was so peaceful, so warm and so nice, but I said, "I'd really love to come, but I can't because I've got work to do."

I also remember saying to them that I had two children and that I wanted to come back to look after my children as well as to work.

And she said to me, "Okay then, we'll send you back and you'll know that this is not a dream, because when you wake up, the first thing you'll see will be the shape of a cross on your door. You'll know the minute you see the cross that what's happened has been a real experience." So I remembered that, and when I woke up I saw on the door a very small cross which was made by sunlight shining through the window. (The window had colonial wooden slats and the cross was made by the sunlight shining through.) The minute I saw it I said, "Oh, my goodness!" I realized that what'd happened was a real experience. After that, miraculously, the infection turned and I got well.

I didn't see my body in the bed during that experience, but in a previous experience I did. On that occasion I'd also just had an operation, and I was being wheeled back to the ward from the operating room. I experienced myself as hovering just below the ceiling of the room, and when I looked down, I could see my body on the trolley. I saw a man with a bald head at one end pushing the trolley and a nurse at the other end, and I watched as they lifted me off and put me into bed. The nurse left the room, and then she came back in and she was carrying a postoperative tray with a white cover across it. The tray was black plastic. She put it on the bedside table, and when the man left the room, she pulled back the cover on the tray and underneath I saw scissors and cotton and bandages and things, and then she put the cover back on and left the room. Next thing I was aware of was waking up, and the first thing I did was look at the bedside table to see if the tray was there, and it wasn't. The same nurse who had put it there came into the room and I said to her, "Where's the tray that was beside the bed?'' She said, ''How did you know there was a tray? You were unconscious.'' I said, ''Oh, I saw you wheel me in—you and a fellow with a bald head.'' She went and told the doctor, and she came in and said, ''Have you been seeing things?'', and I said, ''Well, I know there was a tray there.'' And she said, ''Yes there was.'' I told her everything that was on it, and she said, ''Oh, God!''

One thing I was really aware of during that experience was color—everything was so bright. And I was definitely looking down. There was no way I could have known that that man had a bald patch right on top, except that I was looking down on him.

I definitely wanted to come back [after the NDE], because I felt that I'd been avoiding what I should have been doing with my life. I felt that I was not earning the right to go to that place. I remember saying to the angels, really desperate to get the message across, ''I want to work, I really want to work.'' At that stage I didn't know what the work was that I was going to be doing. I thought I was going to be teaching.

When I found myself conscious in my body again, it felt good, because it was as if I'd been revitalized. And I think that was evident in the fact that I started to get better from then on, whereas up till then I'd been desperately sick. My body started to get better and I felt reenergized and ready for this next big commitment that I knew I'd just made.

I feel I didn't die because I was needed to work in the work I'm doing now. And also to be with my children. My daughter was quite young, about eleven, and my son would have been about fourteen, and I feel that I was really needed at that stage to be their mother.

After the experience, a few weeks later, I told my family about it and they thought I was a bit strange. They told me I was probably suffering from delusions or something. I feel they didn't understand it and it was very hard to explain anyway. I later talked about it to a friend of mine who's a doctor. He finds all this sort of thing fascinating. It's not that he understands—I mean, he comes to me for explanations about spiritual matters—so he was not able to throw any light on it, but it was nice to be able to talk to him and for him not to judge me as being strange.

Before that experience I'd never read anything about it at all. At that time I didn't have any interest in anything psychic or spiritual, nothing at all. I didn't know what the word *psychic* meant.

I've always believed that life goes on after death, but I didn't understand how. It was a bit like a closed school to me. But now I believe we learn so much after death. I believe that death is just a different experience of life. And I believe that we have responsibilities and a lot more growth to undertake after death.

Even before my NDE, I was completely convinced that there was life after death. I knew this for sure because of the experience I had when my other daughter died. My daughter died when she was ten days old. She was in the hospital and I was living about twenty miles away. She'd been operated on and was progressing well. I was to go in the following day to pick her up from the hospital and bring her home. I was really looking forward to it—I had a little outfit picked out and everything ready to go and get her.

I was sound asleep and at two o'clock in the morning I suddenly sat straight up in bed, and I was aware that something had happened. I felt very apprehensive. I didn't know why I sat up, and then I recognized that the spirit had passed over me, letting me know she'd passed on. Twenty minutes later the phone rang and it was the hospital. They said she died at exactly two o'clock—exactly the minute I sat up in bed. So that was my very first connection with a strong belief that there's more to us than just a body, and that in death we are still alive. Since then I've had a lot of experiences to confirm that.

Now my work makes me more interested in death, because I work with a lot of people who are dying. I'm also interested because of the fact that I'm clairvoyant—that happened after that near-death experience. Being clairvoyant, I'm constantly in touch with souls who are on the other side. It sounds ridiculous and my mind says it isn't logical, but it's just like a fact of life for me.

I describe my NDE as absolutely, totally spiritual—not religious, but spiritual. Before that experience, I'd have said that I believed firmly in God, but I wouldn't have said I was a religious person. Now I would say I am a very spiritual person, but I still don't see myself as religious. Before, I would've seen myself as a Protestant, but now I feel less that organized religion has the answers. Today I believe more in spirituality, and I don't feel that it has to be labeled. I feel more that the answers come from within your own being. That experience was a total confirmation for me that God exists.

Before [the NDE], I couldn't strongly believe in psychic phenomena, because I'd only had the one experience with my daughter, yet I knew that there was something there which was rather exciting. Now, of course, I have no doubt whatsoever.

My clairvoyance has increased markedly since the NDE. As a child I had some of what I realize now was clairvoyant experience, although at the time I couldn't label it. I was aware very much of my own third eye. I was about three or four when I first saw my own third eye. And also, when I was about two years of age, I had an experience when I was told that when I grew up and got married, I was going to have a baby girl and she would die. I also saw my husband when I was a child, and when I saw him in real life, I recognized him straightaway.

I have a lot more precognitive visions now than before. Of course, because of the nature of my work, I have a lot of those during my working hours, but I do have precognitive dreams as well, and I take them very seriously. I also get direction in my dreams, and I find I'm understanding more of the symbolism now, so my ability to decipher their meaning has definitely increased.

Before my NDE, I never felt I was in touch with spirits or guides, but now it happens constantly. I guess with me, it's not a matter of me actually visualizing them. I suppose it comes more from feelings—I feel what they're saying to me, or sometimes I actually hear, because I'm clairaudient as well. I actually hear them speaking. But I feel I'm more here for other people's guides—to give information from them to the people who come to see me.

It is also possible to actually see souls as they pass, and to get information from them about issues which relate to their own relatives. For example, this doctor friend of mine came to see me with his wife one night not long ago, and told me that a patient of his had just died. He asked me to tune in and find out whatever I could about that man. So I did, and I told him that he had a toe which was black (and in fact that was true—he had gangrene of the toe), and he'd died of a heart attack. His spirit came through with a very strong message about the fact that he was extremely angry with one of the hospital staff—she wore a yellow uniform and she'd come into his private room while he was dying and gone through his coat, which was hanging up in his locker, and taken money. I described the woman through the words of the soul who told me this, and the doctor knew straightaway the woman concerned. He went to her and confronted her with it, and she admitted that she had, in fact, taken the money. And the soul was satisfied that he'd given the message. There were also personal messages for his family. He told me that he'd come from the north coast, and gave messages about what he wanted done with certain parts of his property etcetera. That is an experience that happens quite a lot when spirits have just passed on. They do come to deliver messages to us still on earth.

If I want to I can tune in to other people, no matter where they are, and get information about whatever. A while ago my sister and I decided to do a little experiment with out-of-body experiences. She was living probably about fifteen miles away. One morning we were talking over the phone about it, and decided to work out a little experiment. So she said, "Okay, I'll just go about what I'm doing and you come and visit me, spiritually, while I'm doing what I'm doing." And she said, "Ring me and tell me what I've been doing." So I did. I traveled consciously, or left my body consciously, and went to her house. When I did, I saw that she was in the laundry. One tub was filled with water and there were red clothes soaking in it, and the other tub was empty. I saw three little children playing with their dogs in the yard out the back. Then I saw them all run through the back door, through the house and into the lounge room. I then saw two of the children chasing a dog and then my sister running in and screaming, "Get that dog out of here!" I also saw her knock herself on the corner of the table in the kitchen as she was chasing the kids. So about twenty minutes later I told her everything that I saw. She couldn't believe it, for it was absolutely one hundred percent what had happened. So after that, we were quite convinced about our out-of-body experiences.

It was quite different from seeing things clairvoyantly. In our experiment I had to will myself to leave my body and travel the distance of about fifteen miles from where I was living to where she was living, and I experienced myself consciously going out of my body. When somebody comes in for a reading, none of that takes place and I'm totally conscious at this level. I'm not leaving my body, but I know I have a knowledge of what other people don't understand about their own lives, or about what they want for their lives, or what direction they should take. I receive information which is given to me in different ways—one is prayer and another is clairvoyance and clairaudience, and another is just like a feeling of just knowing. And there is another way of picking up information, and that is through automatic writing.

I usually tend not to do automatic writing but, for example, I've been working on a television program for quite a few years where the information is given to us via automatic writing. Questions are asked and I write the answers and they are then researched. It is a historical program, based on actual history, so the information we are given leads the researchers to archives and manuscripts and so forth. It's about the early foundations of Australia's history, and it's done by people who are paid to go and research and come up with information. A lot of incredible facts have come out of that.

After my near-death experience, I came to value myself a lot more. I felt that I was more worthy to be loved by myself, although I still felt obliged to attend to my responsibilities, of course—I didn't want to indulge myself too much. But the search for inner meaning began about a year later.

I was teaching at the time in a school where I was librarian, and I had the task of setting up the library. It was a huge, brand-new library, so I was responsible for buying all the books. But I also had some free time. One morning I was sitting in my office when the cleaner came and told me that she was going to have a séance that night. I said, ''What is a séance?'' And she explained to me about how she used the glass and had the alphabet arranged etcetera. So I said, ''Okay, see if you can give me any information about my daughter.'' So she said she'd try. She came back the next afternoon and she had a piece of paper, and on it she had the name of my daughter written. She had no idea that I even had a daughter who died, we'd never spoken about it. She had the baby's name written, Susan Marie Natasha, and the message ''I love you, Mum.'' I nearly passed out. So after that I began to think that there really must be something to all this.

Strangely enough, the following week I had to go to a warehouse to buy books for the library, and they had sent a gentleman to pick me up. He was an elderly man, about seventy. In the glove box of his car (which had no lid on it—it was like an open shelf) there was a book called *Life After Life*. As we were driving along, I said, ''That sounds like an interesting book.'' And he said, ''It's fascinating. Are you interested in life after death?'' And I said, ''Well, I know nothing about it, but I certainly would like to know.'' So he gave me the book. And when we got to the warehouse, he picked out five or six other books on similar topics and gave them to me. That got me started. After that I couldn't stop—I couldn't find out enough. I got a totally new outlook on life.

I knew that I had to keep growing. I knew that I had to find out more, and I also knew I had to give more. The more I discovered, the more I had to give. So it meant I had to change my career. So I left teaching and tried to find an outlet for the knowledge that I had gained. And I found it very difficult to find an acceptable profession where I could pass on my truths without it being too strange. So the best I could do was to look into alternate methods and hypnotherapy, which gave me a label which meant that people could relate to me under that sort of banner. Once that happened, I was able to use my gifts, which I feel were a result of that near-death experience.

There was a lot of strain in my relationships. Everybody thought I'd gone quite peculiar, because I'd left the security of teaching after fifteen years, and I felt quite lost myself while I was redirecting my energy. So my parents thought I was quite irresponsible, and my husband and children didn't understand what I was doing. I have a good relationship with my family now, but that's because I'm at the other end now, and they know that the work I'm doing has proven to be quite useful.

I found that a lot of the friends that had been very necessary for me were no longer necessary, so I just moved away. Also, I find it very lonely, because I can't have really close relationships with people. It's not because they don't understand where I'm coming from—that's not it—it's just that all of my energies go into the work I'm doing, and what's left over I have to give to my family. So I have an isolated life in terms of friendship, which is very sad in a way, but I get a lot of loving support from the people I work for.

I'm much more loving toward people today. I genuinely love people. I have a great amount of empathy for people, and incredibly more patience and tolerance. I used to be very impatient with people, but now I find myself being very patient.

My attitude to learning changed, too, because before that experience, I'd always considered learning to be of the academic nature. And now I feel that that is very valid, but there is another type of learning which to me seems to be even more valid, and that is a learning of spiritual matters gained not so much through what other people can tell you, but through what you can decipher for yourself.

I did actually start studying [after the NDE]. The first thing I did was to enroll at a university to do psychology. But I found myself being very dissatisfied with it. I couldn't accept it, I felt there was so much more. So after six months I left it, because the more I did, the more disgruntled I became. After that I padded around for a bit and wondered what I should be doing and then, strangely enough, one day when I was in the local shopping center, I noticed there was a numerologist who'd set up his stall. My girlfriend encouraged me and so I paid my $2.50, and he typed out a sheet of information for me in which he said things that triggered me off. Eventually out of that I was led to enrolling in the course of natural therapies, which was so much more valid for me. I was able to relate to that so much better than to the formal academic university-type situation.

But while I was studying that course, I also became very aware—I was actually told in a dream that I was going to become clairvoyant, and that I would be in kindergarten stage. Three weeks after that dream, I in fact had my first clairvoyant vision. I didn't know if I should trust that, but more and more situations came up when I was telling strangers truths about themselves. Then I realized that the dream was in fact a direction. And so I started to give readings to the lecturers at college where I was studying. They could see the gift that I had because I was also giving diagnoses as well. I was advised by a couple of them to get out of studying, to get out and into life, and use my gift. So I did. I followed up the natural therapies course with hypnotherapy, and found that very interesting, too. I've worked ever since, and that's about eight years now.

After seeing about two or three people as a hypnotherapist, I realized I shouldn't continue to hide behind that label. And as soon as I started seeing people for healings and readings on their lives, the whole thing just took off, and people come to me now either as somebody who needs to see me as a clairvoyant, or hypnotherapist or a psychic healer. I even work with doctors sometimes. I work with doctors who accept what I'm doing—they still do their thing with a patient, while allowing me to do my thing, too. In particular, with the medical profession, a lot of the work I do is training people not to accept anything that's too drastic or too radical.

Today my life is *extremely* fulfilling! *Unbelievably* fulfilling! *Totally* rewarding! I had no idea that fulfillment at this level was a possibility. I'm totally contented, very rewarded in what I do and I'm just so happy. I shudder to think how it compares with my life before the NDE! Oh, look truly, when I compare myself today with the person I was before this experience, I just can't compare. Really, I'm a different person, totally. I'm just another person altogether. Today I have a real appreciation of how everything is so intricate and so valuable and so beautiful.

C H A P T E R 5

On the Other Side

The otherworld has often been described by near-death experiencers as a "world of light." Entrance into that world of light is an indicator of the deepest kind of near-death experience, and is the privilege of a small proportion of NDErs. Those who do spend time on the other side tell of being in a wondrous light, seeing beautiful landscapes, buildings and even cities. They recount meetings with deceased relatives, pets, luminous beings and even a Being of Light who radiates love and peace. They tell of encounters ranging from fleeting glimpses to long conversations and guided tours. They almost always *want* to stay, even if they do finally have to return.

Hal, a fourteen-year-old schoolboy who suffered three heart attacks one day at school, had an extremely deep and complex experience during which he had an encounter with the Light, saw a city in the distance and was taken into a building called the "archives," within which he had an experience of having "all knowledge." He describes his meeting with the Light:

My friend Tom [Hal's deceased school friend who was acting as his guide] said: "Look, the Light's coming now!"

I could see in the distance a pinpoint of light and it was coming toward me. The Light seemed to be coming from hundreds of miles away, coming at immense speed. And it just kept getting bigger and brighter. It was perhaps the brightest light I've ever seen. As the Light got closer the feeling of peace got even greater. It was a wondrous feeling. And then the Light got very close and I said to Tom, "What am I supposed to do? Do I have to get down on my knees and pray? I've never done anything like this before."

He said, "No, don't worry. You don't have to do anything like that. He'll start to talk to you. You just answer anything he asks you."

The Light came up to me then and spoke to me.

Helen[1] also described speaking with the Light:

It was beautiful where I was going. And I'm sure I saw people, and I recognized my grandmother. And I met this beautiful big Being of Light—it wasn't any form but it was just beautiful, a beautiful golden color. It's indescribable.

I was really happy to go, but then I thought about my little children, two little boys plus the baby, and I really felt I should be a mother to them and bring them up. So I discussed it with the Being of Light. It was really beautiful and he said that I could come back to fulfill my life as a mother. It was just lovely.

A few people have described seeing buildings of

one kind or another. It was Hal's friend Tom who took him into a building called the "archives." Hal describes what happened:

When we went into the building we went first into a big room and there was a corridor in front of us. It only seemed to be about twenty feet long, but as we walked along there still seemed to be twenty feet to go. We kept on going and going. This corridor was alive—it was a living room. It had walls that went up about ten feet and then there were upper wall panels that leaned in toward us. These panels seemed to be beaming knowledge down onto me. As I went through, all this knowledge was coming to me. Everything that was known to mankind was in these archives and it was coming down into my mind. By the time I got to the end I felt I knew everything. But now I can't remember it!!

When we finally were ready to leave, Tom said, "Now I'm going to take all this knowledge away from you. You're not allowed to take that back."

I said, "You can't take it away from me—it's all here in my mind." I knew all languages, everything.

He said to me, "What's the word they use in Afghanistan for red?"

I told him quite readily what the word was. Then he did something and I forgot.

One of the NDErs in Kenneth Ring's study described a similar experience of knowing all languages:

I could hear languages. All languages. Languages that I had never heard before and I could understand them.[2]

And I came across another interesting example

of "knowing everything" quite recently in an interview I did with a teenager who had her experience as a four-year-old child during a tonsillectomy. She described how, while she observed the doctors doing the operation, she felt such compassion for their ignorance. She felt that she, as the spirit of a four-year-old child, was so much wiser, knew so much more than they did.

There are so many aspects of experience on the other side that could be discussed. For example, several of Ring's respondents reported seeing a city of lights and Hal also says that he could look into a city from the archives building. However, more usually, experiencers who reach the other side become aware of the "light," the beauty of which they say is inexpressible. Some describe a radiant landscape, and some even interact with luminous beings, or at times deceased relatives or friends. One dear friend, who nine years ago came close to death in a car accident in which her husband was killed, recently wrote of her experience for the AUSTRALIANDS newsletter:

We died together, he and I, and as entities of energy, we moved together to a place outside of time and space. . . . I became aware of the LIGHT. I struggle to find earth-words to describe it. It is the light-of-being, pulsating from each of us. And the sound! It is the sound-of-being, radiating from each of us to create a community of pure, sacred vibration! . . .

I moved to another plane where my Being expanded until I was One-With-All. It is the ultimate coming Home. There is only Oneness, total belonging. And there is only ecstasy. I knew I wanted to be here where I belonged, forever One with the Light. I was told I must return to earth because I had not completed my work there. I did not want to go, yet I understood many things. My husband would stay and I would go and that was just the way it was. . . .[3]

It is worth allowing Joy to continue the telling of her story since it so movingly illustrates the theme of this book:

I returned to my broken body and earth consciousness. I knew where I had been, I knew my husband was dead, and I knew I would spend the remainder of my life on earth pursuing the irresistible force of that transformation. For nine days I was enveloped in a cocoon of golden light. Unconditional love poured from my heart; I was in a state of grace. Compassion, innate harmony and healing energy were my being. . . .

This near-death experience continues to live daily in my life. I understand that the uncompleted work for which I have been sent back is to share the unconditional love I was so unconditionally given. I know that God is the totality of all life, whether it manifests as Oneness or as trees, grass and people. My body has healed. My grief is not less intense but less frequent. Five years ago I realised that it was no longer appropriate to "hang out up there," out of my body, but that I had to bring that essence into this piece of clay called my body. And that is when the real work began; to address the unfinished business of my life, to learn to become present in my life, to live and die consciously.

In this chapter, five other near-death experiencers share their stories. On the other side Juliet finds herself in a forest where she encounters beautiful people; Shana describes being in a golden world with angelic beings; Mary experiences enfoldment in the Light and an interaction with three luminous beings; Grace finds herself in a gentle landscape surrounded by many deceased relatives; and Janet hears wonderful music and finds herself in the loving presence of the Light.

JULIET

I first heard about Juliet from a mutual friend who had attended some of her workshops. After speaking on the telephone, I went to her apartment to do the interview. Juliet is a tall, slim woman, with pale skin and a shock of black, frizzy hair. She is very softly spoken and gentle in attitude. After spending a couple of hours with her that first day, I gained the impression that she was a deeply spiritual, sensitive and caring person. However, once again, as with so many of the women I interviewed, this sensitivity and gentleness should not be confused with weakness. Juliet is a person of considerable capability and strength.

Juliet was forty-six years old when she had her second near-death experience, and at that time she was already working as a psychic healer. We recorded our interview seven years later.

It was under surgery—a bladder repair operation. I was in the operating room and I could feel myself going to sleep. Then there was a noise like wings flapping—that's the only noise I can think of to describe what I heard. I haven't actually heard a huge bird with wings flapping, but that's the sort of noise it was—not actually a roaring, but more of a flapping. And then there was this feeling of being pulled very quickly along. I've read that people go down a tunnel and there's light at the end of the tunnel, but it wasn't actually a tunnel—it was more like just in space. There was no enclosure, there was just a feeling of wholeness (tears). It's hard to explain. And then I was conscious of a number of what to me seemed to be men. And I was in a very beautiful forest. But I've never seen a forest like that, it was (tears) so beautiful, with huge trees, immense trees. They were so tall! And there was a clearing, we were at a clearing, and it seemed to be very light. It was just so powerful. It was a magnificent light—it wasn't like this—it was just so purely white. And these beautiful people were standing around and I said (tears), "Thank goodness I'm here!" I said, "I thought I was coming before but I didn't make it. But I'm home now." And they kind of just looked at me. There wasn't really any verbal interchange. It didn't feel as though anyone really spoke to me, but the feeling was, "No, Juliet, you have to go back. You've got a lot more to do." And that was it. I just remember waking up. I don't remember coming back or leaving. But when I woke up, there was a wonderful feeling of peace—just knowing. You don't know what you know but you know something (laughs). And such a feeling of tranquillity. The feeling that it's okay, everything's okay. It was an overwhelming feeling, and it's stayed with me.

The next morning, one of the nurses was walking past—she'd just come on duty. She was walking past the door and then she came back and looked in. She came over to me and said, "What's happened to you?" She said, "I was walking past, and when I looked in, I could see this glow around you." I told her what'd happened. I didn't know whether she was going to laugh or not. And she said, "Yes, I believe you—it happens." And she said, "You just looked different," and she talked with me.

It's very difficult to put the experience into words, because it's about feeling. It really doesn't have anything to do with verbal conversation—it's beyond that. Even now, when I think about it, I still get emotional.

I actually had another NDE five years earlier. I don't remember being with people that time, but I certainly remember going out and being in light, and the wonderful feeling of peace.

That time there was great panic in the operating room. I'd told them that I was allergic to anesthetic, but they'd taken no notice. I remember them saying, "Her breathing, her breathing, watch her breathing," and that was while I was going under, before I'd actually gone into unconsciousness. They were saying, "Watch her breathing, watch her breathing, she's breathing strange," but I didn't really take a lot of notice, because it's happened every time I've had surgery (and I've had a lot of surgery). Then I was watching the whole thing. I don't remember popping out, but I was there—not right up on the ceiling, just sort of midway.

While I was up there I could see very clearly. Someone started doing things to my chest and then they got those electric shockers. (I was bruised both times when I came out from those experiences.) It all seemed a bit unnecessary and not particularly interesting. I thought, "Oh, it doesn't matter, it's okay." And then I left that mundane scene behind (laughs). For a while I just seemed to be in space, and then I went into the white light. I don't remember encountering anyone that first time, but the same feeling of peace and tranquillity came. There didn't seem to be anyone to say, "Hey, go back" (laughs), but it was wonderful. And then I just woke up.

I'm sure I didn't die on either of those occasions because I still had a lot of work to do. I had to get on with it and do what I had to do. I was already working in this area, and in the second experience I felt the message was, "You're doing well, Juliet, but you have to go back and do some more." I feel a strong sense of purpose now, and I feel very fulfilled in what I do.

• • •

I don't think I've ever been afraid of death. As a child I lived on a farm, and there it was natural. It just wasn't an issue. Now I have no fear at all (laughs). If anything, I've got a death wish now (laughs). Not actually a death wish, but I do look forward to it.

Suicide, of course, that's different. Suicide is something that has tempted me in the past, but I wouldn't dream of doing it now. I know what's there, but I also know that I had to come back for a reason.

Although I had no fear of death before my NDEs, I don't think I had any particular interest in death either. But now, in the work I do, I find I can help others to lessen their fear of death or dying, sometimes just by helping them to look at a past life or something like that. They do it themselves—I'm just there as a catalyst.

[The NDE] was a fully spiritual experience for me. As a child I was brought up in the Church of England, and went to a Church of England boarding school where I spent a lot of time in the chapel—I was very religious. But then I began to find that religion was too restricting, there wasn't enough scope for expanding and looking into other things. I then looked at all sorts of religions, but ended up with just being me. Now I know that there is a higher energy, a universal force, and that it works through everything and everyone, and that as long as we take responsibility for ourselves, we're not going to hurt or do damage to anything or anyone. Today I meditate and I talk to God. I'm conscious that that energy is there and I communicate. I ask for help if I need it, and I try not to worry about my problems. I try to leave my life to the care of the universal provider.

I've had many psychic experiences. Even as a child, people used to laugh at me because I was always "away with the fairies." I guess as soon as I was out the door on my own, I *was* in a different world, but I never did see fairies. I used to make things, and I'd talk to them, and I had a "friend" that was always with me—not a real friend, but a real friend to me. And we talked to the animals, communicated with animals. Animals and birds would just come to me. But about three years ago I'd been working in the daytime and I had the group at night, and I was feeling a bit tired, so I thought, "I'll just go and lie on the bed for about twenty minutes." I'd just stretched out on the bed and I was very tired, and I just sort of closed my eyes, but for some reason I opened my eyes again and looked across the room. On top of the TV in the bedroom is quite a big jade Buddha, and next to it there's a vase with some dried flowers, and there was this glow. I thought, "Hmm, that's a bright light. That's weird!", but I just lay back. Then as I watched it seemed to start to sparkle, because there were little flashes—blue, blue mauve and silver, a lot of silver. And it was flashing and it was getting brighter and brighter, and then it went into the form of an actual fairy—the wings and all! I thought, "That's a big fairy!" (laughs). It was just leaning, or almost sitting, on top of the Buddha. I could see right through, but the outline was there in this haze. And then it was gone. Two days later I was in another room making notes. I was concentrating and I sort of glanced across at a bowl of flowers on the table and there it was again. I was so surprised (laughs).

But one very strong experience happened about seventeen years ago. I had just left my marriage and I was in another relationship. We went for a drive one night, and we were sitting in the car talking. And suddenly this voice screamed at me, "Go, Juliet, go!" And I didn't question it, I just said, "We've got to go!" And Geoff immediately turned the ignition on and I looked through the window, and coming across, from four panel vans, was a group of guys with chains, tire irons, all that sort of stuff. Luckily Geoff didn't say, "Why, what's wrong?" He just immediately reacted and we took off. And then they chased us and they ran back to the panel vans and chased us in the vans. It was a hell drive out, because they followed and tried to cut us off. It would have been death, I imagine. I feel I didn't have to go that way, you know. I was told to get moving, and we moved! It proves that if we listen, we'll be guided. This voice was like you sitting there and screaming at me, it was just so loud and it saved our lives.

I have out-of-body experiences from time to time. Sometimes they just happen, but I can also induce them. In meditation, when I'm very tired, it's fairly easy. The energy input and output is through my feet, more than anywhere else, and I feel the pull. I know it's different for everybody, but for me it's the feet, and I feel the energy going *vroom,* out like that, and it's almost like a draining, in a way, but it's revitalizing as well. Sometimes I'm conscious of just floating, but I don't work terribly much in that sort of way. More often I tell myself to go somewhere, and go there. I always do it with a purpose, I never just go looking round—I can't be bothered.

If I'm concerned about someone, whether it be family or friend, or if someone gives me a name, I then go to that person. For instance, about six years ago a friend tried to commit suicide, and he was in a coma for two months. A daughter, a friend and myself had been constantly in and out of intensive care. This day we were getting very tired, and so we decided we'd better go home and get some rest. I came home and I was under the shower, and I thought, "What else can I do to help?" And the answer was, "Just go to him, go to his body. Go and make him breathe." So I then lay on the bed, and I went into his body, and I started to breathe for him. After a while I got up and went to the phone.

I called the hospital and said, "Could you tell me how he is?" The sister said, "He's just the same." So I thought it hadn't worked (laughs). So I went to bed and I just left it. I thought, "Oh well, I'm not supposed to heal him."

But the next morning when we went to the hospital, the sister said he'd improved. I asked her, "When did he start breathing," and she gave the time. Apparently she'd left the phone after I called, went to check on him and found he was breathing.

My life today is rather full, but my one real interest is in doing what I can to help other people find themselves. Sure, I enjoy going out and socializing, but only to a point. It seems so superficial, so nothing. I can't be bothered sitting and talking to people on "social" topics. I like to sit with people who have similar interests. I guess it's selfish or narrow, in a way, but it's important to continue growing.

I think the most significant change to come about for me since the NDE is that now I have confidence. It confirmed what I already believed, so now it doesn't matter whether people believe me or not. That's not the issue anymore. I don't feel I have to prove anything. Now I have the confidence to go about my work and not worry what others think. The near-death experience has had the effect of giving me more peace in my life, more compassion for other people, and their needs and feelings. Just thinking about it brings more joy and beauty.

SHANA

I had accompanied my husband to the television studio where he was to be interviewed for a weekend magazine program. In the green room we were introduced to Shana, who was also waiting to appear on the same program, to discuss her work with dolphins. We chatted for a while until the show began. During her interview I was astonished to hear Shana mention, just in passing, how her life had been changed by nearly dying. Of course I immediately suspected that she'd had a near-death experience, and later she confirmed it was true.

Afterward we drove her to a friend's place. Along the way we talked about her NDE and arranged to meet again if ever we passed by her town on the north coast of New South Wales. About six months later Shana was included on my northern "interview itinerary."

Shana has a look of fragility about her. She is slim and fine-boned, with wispy blond hair and clear blue eyes. We spent a winter's morning with her in her house, which is situated close to the water. We sat on the floor in a room filled with sunshine to record our interview.

Shana was twenty-three and training as a nurse at the time of her NDE, but by the time we spoke twenty-one years later, she was "working with the consciousness of whales and dolphins."

I was in the hospital for a very simple kidney operation, but I went into shock because of an allergic reaction. I was in constant pain, and they couldn't stop the pain, and they couldn't stop the contractions. And they had to take me back to the operating room, and I had three cardiac arrests, all from shock. And I saw a whole movie of my life—everything. It was incredible. I remember at the time being amazed at the things that I'd forgotten. I saw everything from day one right up to the present day—every single little thing. I didn't feel judged at all—it was fantastic. It was like I was watching this movie of my life, it was fascinating.

That was great, but then I had the feeling of all my senses closing down—just the whole body, shutting down. It was very weird. And then I was outside my body, and I was watching everybody working on me.

They knew I was Australian (I was in England at the time) and they were very sorry that this was happening, and it was near Christmastime, too. I just felt such incredible compassion for them. And I was looking at my body—it was five and a half stone [about 75 pounds] and was really skinny. I knew that my body was finished—I realized the limitations of it. And I was watching this little body and I thought, "Well, it was a good little body in its time, but it's finished."

And I could see my mother out in the hall of the hospital in Sussex, England, and I could see my father in Australia—I could see everybody I was connected to. It was just one big global thing. And the doctors and the nurses were working on me. And there was this incredible feeling of compassion that I'd never felt before. I have felt it since, but I'd love to have it all the time. And I was just letting everybody know that I was okay. It was just incredible seeing everybody—my father in Australia (he didn't know it was happening), my mother (she was very concerned) and the doctor, whose wife was dying of cancer. I felt a special compassion for him because this shouldn't have been happening—this was like a disaster for him. It just shouldn't have happened, and I felt real compassion for him.

And while I was up there it was like I was in this golden world, this incredible golden world filled with Christ light. I just felt I was part of it all, part of the whole, that this was where I belonged, that this was the truth. And there were all these beings, angels, angelic, luminous beings and this feeling of *total* love. And the one thing I got when I was up there was that my task was to serve, that the only purpose for humans is to serve the planet and to live life absolutely to the fullest. I knew that was the way to get back there. I knew I would never get back there by committing suicide. But that was for me personally, it wasn't a general statement for every person. There are some people I know who've committed suicide—it's a path for some people. It's just not my path, it was definitely not my path. My path was to come back here and to serve. And it took me forever.

I was only twenty-three, just an Australian traveling overseas. Before the operation I wasn't really conscious of anything much—I was thinking about getting married to an Englishman and staying in England. But after that, I didn't want to get married anymore. I mean, I didn't want to live that life. I came back and I didn't know *how* to be, but I didn't want to be how I was. It was a case of "I don't know what I want but I don't want this." And to understand what service meant, that took me another ten years.

I have no idea how I got back—I was just suddenly back. And I was angry that I was back, it was a shock. I was deeply shocked because my body was quite painful. And after that, I went through another two months when they thought I would be incontinent, and the thought of that at twenty-three was *really* . . . ! I was saying, "Thanks a lot, this is great, thanks!" (laughs).

So it took me quite a while for everything to come together—to get used to the fact that I was back, to work out what the message was, to realize what it meant to say my life was to be of service. And all the feelings—it took me a while for them all to come together. I'd had this incredible expansion of consciousness—I knew that where I'd been was how it really was. It was the truth of the world.

I didn't mention it at all, ever, until I did a Buddhist meditation retreat five years later. They described it right, except for the fact that they said only saints and gurus go out through the top, and all the rest of us leave through the feet. I went out through the top. Then I didn't talk about it again till much, much later, and I was very careful who I talked to.

Later on I went through all sorts of things trying to work out what it meant to serve. I went through a self-denial stage—you know, like everything that I had, I had to give away. I thought that I shouldn't have anything. But eventually I worked out that that wasn't service, because it made me very rigid. And I went through a lot of things until I eventually came to know that service was, for me, to understand myself—that I first had to love myself before I could love others.

Before my NDE I'm not sure I actually gave death much thought. But I *was* into reincarnation, because I did children's nursing, and that was the only thing that made any sense of children suffering and dying. But now I think when we die, we become unlimited, if we're willing to become unlimited.

I have a lot of psychic experiences, although I suppose it depends on what you call psychic. I sometimes spontaneously have out-of-body experiences, but I did go through a period of doing it voluntarily. I'd be dreaming about certain people, and I'd actually be there with them. They'd call me up the morning after, and say they'd seen me. It happened quite a lot.

I also get precognitive flashes—while I'm awake and in dreams. The dolphins in a nearby aquarium, for instance, they told me they were going to Queensland the night before they did, and why. They were transported.

I have a very strong appreciation of the natural world. I think I always had it, but I think I became much more conscious of it after the NDE, much more aware that everything in the living world is conscious.

Six years ago (1983), the dolphins came into my head in a dream, thousands of them. I mean, I didn't have a clue, and every time I closed my eyes, they'd come into my head. And within a week people'd given me all sorts of information. And I thought, warm-blooded, air-breathing animals just like us, with a bigger brain, and their society, and all that sort of stuff, so I became quite interested. And then I went to New York and dolphins kept coming into the work I was doing, and I thought this was really bizarre. And on the way back I saw a dolphin and thought, "What's this all about?" It answered, "Thank goodness you asked! We all live in the one brain, the one mind. We are the communication experts on the planet. All you have to do is open up your reality—out of your three-dimensionality—and we're there to help you."

Since then I've studied dolphins and whales through working with them in Florida. I went there just to see if the communication could be opened up, and I found that there was so much information there. Everybody can have an experience. And I've found that the hospice and autistic people are particularly helped by them. So now I'm setting up a center here on the north coast. It's a giant undertaking, but it's all going smoothly. There's always enough money to cover whatever is needed. I've made a commitment to set it up so there will be such a resource. But we will go beyond even that in the next five years.

Our first aim is to upgrade human consciousness. There is an educational purpose—it is essential for humans to be aware of dolphins and whales and their communication. They're very remarkable, and we want people to know that. The research center and laboratory will bring all the researchers together, and every question they've got will be answered for them. We will work with the wild dolphins.

There's been a total shift in focus for me since my NDE. On a personal level, I think it's shifted from a material sense of well-being to a sense of well-being from inside. I'm not at all motivated by material success now—it doesn't worry me at all. Sometimes I have it and sometimes I don't have it, and I don't care which way it is. The important thing is to serve. My task is to serve the planet by opening communication. I used to work in the ecology movement, but I decided I could be more effective in doing what I'm doing now—working on the communication thing, working for no separation.

Mary

I first met Mary when she approached me after a talk I had given at a conference. Some weeks later she welcomed me warmly to her small, comfortable apartment in a northside suburb of Sydney. I shall always remember her kindly concern for my welfare that day—as we parted she warned me to take care not to overdo things, that I was already getting overtired. Since that first meeting, we have met on many occasions, and now that she is living in another state, we still maintain our friendship over that greater distance. She has become the Queensland organizer for AUSTRALIANDS, helping to arrange meetings and often making herself available to near-death experiencers who want to speak with someone. In more recent times, she has even begun giving talks on near-death experiences—something she didn't think she would ever be able to do.

Mary is a small, energetic woman of very youthful appearance. She has short, dark, curly hair that is slightly threaded with gray, round sparkling eyes and a flawless complexion. She has a mischievous chuckle and an unflappable way of dealing with whatever arises. She seems endlessly willing to put herself out for others, and is much loved and appreciated by those around her.

Mary was fifty-eight years old and already working as a healer when she had her NDE. Our interview was recorded eight years later.

Leading up to the experience, I had been doing a tremendous amount of flying, which had adversely affected my veins. I continued to have a lot of trouble with my veins, so my doctor suggested that I should have them stripped. So I went in for a stripping—a simple operation—and had a cardiac arrest. It turned out I was allergic to the anesthetic. It was the most wonderful experience!

I didn't see my own body but I knew that I was out of it, because I felt so light—there was nothing dragging me. And the tunnel bit for me was just like what I imagine it must feel like being ejected from an aircraft—just *whoosh*—into the light! It's very difficult to put into words, but the light was wholly enfolding. I was in it and it was in me. It was a sort of oneness of light. And there were three beings there—they were all light, too. There was a recognition, a totally different recognition from what happens when you meet people for the first time and feel that you know them—it wasn't that kind of recognition. It was more a feeling of belonging, a sort of knowing. And they communicated with me and imparted certain information which was to be used for the benefit of other people later on.

I didn't know where I'd gone—I knew that I'd gone somewhere, but I really wasn't sure which dimension I was in. There was no conception of time whatsoever. It was so peaceful, yet not static. It was a total "livingness." I certainly didn't want to return to where I came from.

At that stage there was an awareness of what the light was. I knew it was God, a force, whatever—I can't put a name to it. These three beings also shone. It was strange—they had faces, but they didn't have faces, and they were luminous. Luminosity, that's the word to describe them. In a way I felt it was the same as love, but I can't call it love. It wasn't a subjective feeling—it was a lighting up, right through everything. It was there, it was here, inside, outside, everywhere. And it was total love, enfolding. I can't really separate the light out. Everything was luminous, and the light was just totally enfolding. I had the feeling of being completely at one with everything that was going on around me. I didn't feel at all dead. I felt totally alive, (laughs) much more vibrant. And I had no wish to leave.

I came back because I knew I hadn't finished what I'd come to do. I wasn't told that, but I knew. I remember the light gradually becoming dimmer, but it didn't leave me inside. It's still with me. I can't remember coming down a tunnel or anything like that. I just remember the light becoming dimmer, and then a gradual awakening in a painful body. When I came to properly, everything somehow seemed too hard, and yet a lot of that luminosity stayed with me. I still felt glowing inside.

The doctors apparently had had a lot of trouble getting my heart to go and keep going. And the following morning, one doctor came around and apologized for killing me! (laughs). Well, he didn't actually say ''killing'' me. And then the anesthetist came and apologized. So it was all quite amusing.

The main reason I didn't die was because I had more work to do. When I recovered I was asked to work in the hospice. In any case I was already seeing a lot of people who were dying, especially a lot of cancer patients. That experience meant a lot. When you're dealing with people who are dying, it helps them to know that you know what you're talking about. It's all very well reading a book about it, but face-to-face, with physical contact, and eye contact, it makes all the difference to have been there.

I never did talk about it with my doctor, because he was a very nice man, very caring, but very orthodox, and it would have been dismissed as a hallucination, or some other fancy name. So I share it with people who are dying, and occasionally with friends, but normally only when they ask questions. It's surprising how many people bring the subject up.

I hadn't really read a lot on the topic—some of the theosophical stuff—but any book you read is just purely intellectual. It cannot possibly resemble the experience, because it is so intimate and so personal. I mean, you can understand something intellectually, but it doesn't have any impact. Before [the NDE] I knew, of course intellectually, that my inner being, my spirit, would not die. It would just go into another dimension. That was great, but it was all in the head. I wasn't afraid of the thought of death, not really, it never worried me. I was afraid of dying in pain, yes, but these days that doesn't happen either. Now I have *no* fear of death. I knew of a six-year-old girl who was dying of cancer, and her parents were distraught. She said to them one day, "Stop worrying, I'm all right. I know where I'm going." That's how I feel.

I would never commit suicide, but I feel great compassion for anyone who does, because those who go over as a result of suicide just have to come back to finish what they didn't finish this time.

I definitely don't consider my NDE to be a religious experience, but it was very spiritual. Before that experience I was not religious and I'm still not a churchgoer. Of course, I went to Sunday school as a child (I was baptized into the Church of England), but really it all seemed so totally irrelevant to life, to living life. It's just man-made dogma.

I was already meditating before that experience, and I am still meditating today. I pray, for other people, but it's not like orthodox prayer, it's more like a tuning in. I believe there is a Creator, there must be, but I don't have any vision of the creator as a human being. I say God because it's such a convenient word—God is both male and female, the two main principles of energy. I identify the Light as God, pure Light, with a capital *L*.

• • •

I've had many psychic experiences, both before and since [the NDE], but I tend not to use them unless it's in a healing. If someone is in trouble, there is an ability to look into their heart. People come to me, usually when they've been given up on by the doctors. Their problems can be mental, spiritual, emotional or physical. What I do is channel healing energies that are there for anyone to use. First I look to see if they're meant to have this healing. I check to see whether the angel of death is around, because it's not possible to go against the spirit of that person. *It* knows perfectly well what is needed, and what's going to happen, but the conscious mind often doesn't. So that has to be cleared up first. If that being is present, then I just channel comfort, and hopefully peace, but if that person is open to healing and there's no reason why they shouldn't be healed, I channel the healing energy.

I'm sure there are spirit guides around, but I go direct to the source because I think that bypasses any possible negative influences. Maybe I go *through* them—I think they may act as transformers, because channeling pure God energy through a physical body would probably blow us apart. Occasionally I will work directly with someone's spirit guide—for instance, I do have a friend who has a very strong spirit guide, so I do it with her.

I am much more self-confident these days, and I am much clearer on my life purpose since my NDE. I now do much more work in the healing area, and I wasn't working in the hospice before my NDE. I suppose I should be retired at my age—I do a lot of things, I work as a volunteer for various spiritually focused organizations, as well as doing the healing. But I'm also more tolerant with myself. If I feel very tired these days, I'll just drop everything and relax. We women have been conditioned to keep going, to put other people first, to not think of ourselves, but we have to. I try to look after myself physically. I'm fairly conscious of my diet—I've been vegetarian since 1975—and I walk every day. I don't drink, smoke or take any drugs—I suppose I take a headache pill about once every three months. And I only ever see a doctor once a year for a checkup. I like to go dancing, I love music and I love to see friends. We go out to dinner and we have great get-togethers.

I have no interest in material concerns. I've given away all my material things. I would only work hard for money for a specific purpose, like going overseas. What I really love is the natural world. I do appreciate nature, and people, in fact the whole of life—to look at somebody's garden, or just to smell a rose. I've always been pretty much in tune with nature—I spent my childhood in the country—but it's deepened since the NDE.

I suppose the most significant change for me since my NDE is the feeling I now have about death—the absence of any kind of fear. Before, I was afraid—perhaps of physical pain, or of being alone. It hasn't bothered me since.

Grace

I received a telephone call from Grace after she read a feature about my research in a weekend news magazine. It just happened that I was planning to drive south to Melbourne the following week to do some more interviews, so we arranged to make contact when I arrived. We eventually met at her office and walked to a bistro close by where we talked over lunch. There was a lot of talk and emotion, but little eating was done.

Soon after that meeting, Grace moved and changed her job, and I lost contact with her. It was not until I gave a public lecture in Melbourne following the publication of Reborn in the Light *that I heard from her again. She attended that talk and we have been in contact many times since.*

Grace is now the convenor of the Melbourne branch of AUSTRALIANDS. The very exciting inaugural meeting was held in her home in 1992. She has already made herself available to many near-death experiencers in her locality, and is eager to organize an "outreach" service for hospitals and hospices, with the aim of serving the needs of experiencers who want to talk about their NDEs with someone who understands.

Grace is of medium height, with short, dark, wavy hair and bright, dark eyes. She speaks softly and quickly, and shows a lively curiosity about life's mysteries. At the time of her NDE she was thirty years old and we recorded our interview fourteen years later.

I was in labor, for the first time, and it was an extremely difficult labor. I was thirty and the cervix wasn't dilating properly, and nothing was happening. This had just been going on and on and on, and it was excruciating. I was starting to drift in and out of consciousness and they were getting very panicky. They kept coming in and listening to the fetal heart and checking my pulse. I think that's fairly normal, but all of a sudden there seemed to be a lot of panic and they were wheeling things in, and my husband was shooed out, and I was sort of drifting in and out, and suddenly I wasn't there anymore. I mean, up until then there'd been an awareness of what was going on around me, even though I'd been drifting in and out of blackness. But the last thing I remember before I did move, or had the sensation of movement, was, "We're losing her!" Then suddenly I was somewhere else.

I recall a sensation of movement out beyond myself, like I'd left something behind. And I seemed to move through a portal. There was a glow, but I didn't seem to stop and think, there was no thought, there was no "will I, won't I?" Just suddenly, I found myself in a place, and it was a real place, and I was there. I was standing just beyond the portal and I looked around me. There was an intensity of color. It was a green, an intense emerald green. It was like, there were gentle rolling hills, there were no crags, no sharp edges, nothing that was cruel, nothing that was other than gentle. The sky was intense blue, the scene was gently rolling. (I know you've heard this before, but that's what it was.) And there seemed to be figures, grouped, almost a theatrical grouping, like a stage set. And at first they were just amorphous, shadowy figures and I was peripherally but intensely aware of a grouping on my right, ahead of me, but I hadn't really looked at it. I knew it was there but it was not impinging on my consciousness too much at that stage—I was too busy looking the other way. And as I looked one of the figures seemed to resolve itself, and I thought, "I know that face," and I suddenly realized, "Oh God, it's my aunty Hannah," who died eleven years ago. And then I saw my uncle Abraham, who died before I was born, and I knew them. They were not speaking, their mouths weren't moving, but they were there, and they were sort of there for me. I knew they were there to see me, and they knew me, even though they'd never met me. (I'm going to end up crying.) My granny, who I'd never met, my grandfather, just all the people I've never known and even those I'd known a bit who'd died many years before, or who'd even died recently, and they were there. Anyway, then I turned and I looked at this figure standing next to me—it was my father.

(My dad died when I was sixteen. I was a very rebellious teenager and we were always at loggerheads. And the day he died, we were moving—we'd sold the house and we were going to move into a flat—and he and I had a towering row and I said to him, "I hate you," and did the normal teenage ugly thing. Anyway, he went to the flat with the movers for the last time, saying he'd come back and get me later on. I was waiting for Daddy to come back and the afternoon wore on and there was no sign of him. It was growing dusk when I saw a police car going past. Suffice to say Dad had had a coronary. He died very suddenly, there was no saying good-bye, there was no chance to say, "Dad, I'm really sorry, I didn't mean that. I do love you." It was just . . . he was gone. And I never really was able to mourn properly—I was sort of dashed off to Sydney to live with my mother. It was all very practical: "Now, don't cry, you'll be all right." But I always had this terrible sense that I never had a chance to say good-bye, or a chance to just say "I'm sorry.")

And then standing in that place, it went through my mind, "Is this real or is this my imagination, because it's what I want to have happen?" It's really peculiar, but I actually thought that: "Am I doing this within myself because it's what I want?" And then Dad spoke to me, although there was no speaking—his mind spoke to me. And he said, "No, honey" (because that was his name for me). He said, "Honey, you're not imagining, it's not coming from you, you're with me and this is our time to talk." Anyway, we talked, laid the ghosts to rest. And I looked down and there was my dog Lucky. He died when I was very young, and he was just there. Of course now if I was to go to the same place, my German shepherd would be there, too. I'm quite looking forward to seeing Razzy again. Sounds crazy, doesn't it?

I didn't have any sense of time, I don't know how long it was for, but we talked about all sorts of things. And I said to him, "You must wonder what I've been doing, or you must sometimes feel angry with me." And he said, "No. Here, what goes on in the world has no meaning." He said, "We're here to care for you, we're here to take you on." And then there was a sense of drawing back, and I panicked and said, "Dad, I don't want to go!'' He said, ''You have to go, it's not your time yet, you must go back. You're going to have a son, and you'll have to bring this boy up, bring him up by yourself.'' Then Dad told me my marriage was going to break up. (We'd only been married just a year!) And I remember saying, ''Dad, I don't want that to happen. I always thought that when I got married, it wouldn't happen.'' It was a very intense feeling. I said, ''Dad, I don't want to go—I want to stay with you. Let me stay with you.'' I was most distressed, I didn't want to go back.

He sent me back. He told me that he would be there, he would be there again for me. And I seemed to be moving back quickly, like, there was no sense of travel, but just I was there. And he repeated again, ''You're going to have a boy.'' Then the panic: I thought, ''My God, I haven't picked a boy's name!'' And then I came through, I was there in the delivery room again, and I was crying. My husband was allowed back in, and I was sobbing and sobbing, and I was exhausted. I was just sobbing, with the tears running down my cheeks, and I said, ''I was just with my dad and I had to come back. I tried and tried to stay, but I couldn't.'' John said, ''You're just imagining things.''

Anyway, many hours later, my son was born by cesarean section. They'd apparently lost my pulse at the time. John and my mother were outside, and they were practically in mourning because they had been told, ''She's going, we're losing her.''

I feel an incredible spiritual link with Dad. I don't really feel that death has done anything. He more or less intimated that the way we judge ourselves in the world is not the way they judge. Even though they know what's happened, with our thoughts or whatever, there are no judgments. I didn't feel judged at all. It was almost unemotional. It was the daddy that I knew, but he wasn't making jokes or being affectionate or anything—there was just a complete total love—and it was the same with some of the others.

I couldn't talk about it. I did try many years later, but it was terribly hard. Twice I tried to tell people, but I felt very uncomfortable about it.

It's as though a part of me has been changed. My whole outlook on life has changed so drastically. Before that time I'd always been scared of death, terrified of going into a world of pain. I used to think you'd have the sensation of suffocating, choking, pain. I really didn't know, but I was terrified. But now I know you go to that place. Now I believe death is just another part of human development—like, you're born, you live, you marry, you have children, you die—it's just another step on the road. I'm still formulating ideas—I'm not sure exactly what happens. I certainly don't believe that all those people stand around there for eternity, but I don't really know what they do. That's something I guess that I'll find out when I get there. But I'm not frightened at all.

Up until the time of that experience, I'd been fascinated by the esoteric or, rather, the mystical. I'd searched down many paths. I'd read widely on Buddhism, studied Catholicism and looked into all sorts of different areas—for instance, spiritualism. But after that experience, I felt I had the answer. I was brought up as a Jew, but now I'm not interested in names and tags anymore. I now believe the most important thing is how I feel about myself, how much I like myself, how much I care about the people around me and the world I live in.

Many strange things have happened since that time, uncanny things, like knowing when someone was going to die. Once I was driving along with my son and, just out of the blue, I said, "I think that within twenty-four hours

Penny's father could be 'somewhere else.' " The following morning Penny called me and said that her father had died. I mean he'd been perfectly okay! And that really freaked out my son. (All the psychic experiences have happened since he was born.)

I feel very looked after now, and guided. I've found myself saying to people, "You don't ever need to make a decision, you never need to think about it, decisions make themselves." I never make decisions anymore—I just hand the problems over and wait for the result. That doesn't mean I've found life easy. If anything, life has been terribly difficult, terribly. But being guided is a help. For instance, a strange thing happened just after my husband and I split up. I had an accident, and about three years later I was still waiting for the settlement. My husband had gone through every penny my father had left me, as well as running up an enormous debt. I was hoping that the money I'd get from that accident would perhaps replace, in part, the money that I'd had from Dad. Anyway, one night my son was in bed and I was walking down from the front of the house into the kitchen—I didn't bother to turn the light on—and as I walked in the door my glance sort of went over toward the window and there was a man sitting there. I looked again and he was still there. He was definitely sitting in the window. I sort of zipped through into the kitchen, and switched on the light and went there again, and of course there was nothing there. But it wasn't as though I'd just glanced over—I'd stood and stared. I said, "Who's there?" I was terrified. There was a big Indian vase there, so it couldn't possibly have been a real person in the window.

The man had a hat on, and Dad always used to wear a business suit with a hat, but I thought, "Don't be so stupid." Anyway, a couple of days later, the compensation case was settled, and life changed—until then it had been such a struggle. There was a sense of Dad giving me back my security. The funny thing was that when the money did come through, it equaled exactly what I originally got from Dad. It was weird.

If you could have known me, the sort of person I was before! I've never been a bad person, or immoral, or anything like that, but I was totally irresponsible—not bad, just impulsive. If I wanted to do something, I'd do it. But after that experience, I had a mission, I was given a job to do. It's as simple as that. Up until then, life was aimless—I was living for myself but I came back with a sense of purpose. Suddenly I had to bring up this child alone, I had a mission, a responsibility. I had a reason to be, a reason to do everything. I'd never held a job down. I'd knocked around and traveled all over the place and nothing meant anything. But after, it was just completely different. It was like pulling up a shade, and looking outside or . . . I can't explain it. I just completely changed. Overnight. Suddenly I became a very responsible adult person, and I remember my mother saying, "Something has changed you so much." I tried to tell her about it, but she just said, "Don't be silly!"

My lifestyle today is responsible and very caring. I'm now a personnel consultant, and I have a reputation for being very different from other consultants—very, very empathic. Without people telling me, I seem to understand what they're trying to say. And that's not trumpet sounding, but just an understanding. I think I get more out of what I'm doing because I'm helping. I'm doing something for other people rather than just doing something for me.

After my near-death experience I didn't just grow up—the fabric of my being was rewoven.

Janet

I had heard about Janet from a mutual friend. After talking on the phone a couple of times, it was agreed that, on the return leg of our trip to Victoria, my husband and I would spend the night at Oakdale Sanctuary, the spiritual retreat center she and her husband had established in the Snowy Mountains.

We had been driving for many hours by the time we found ourselves at the turnoff to Oakdale. The narrow dirt road wound around the side of hills green with undergrowth and at times heavily wooded. We could see a stream following a similar path along the valley floor. We passed huge cliff faces, and as we finally approached the house we could see below, on a flat area down by the river, a magnificent stand of oak trees.

Janet and Joe welcomed us warmly and, after settling us into our room, showed us around. As we sat outside talking a baby kangaroo hopped along the veranda, hoping to share in our afternoon tea. (They had apparently raised it since its mother was killed while it was still in the pouch.) After a while Janet and I went inside to record our interview. A couple of hours later we emerged to join the others, and conversation continued long into the night, to be resumed yet again the next morning over breakfast.

Janet is of average height with shoulder-length brown hair and big, round, expressive eyes. She is a warm, loving woman who has an aura of peace about her. She has a ready humor and engaging chuckle. My impression was that she was totally dedicated to her work at Oakdale. How this situation originally came about, and continues to develop, is one of the more remarkable features of Janet's story.

Janet had her experience when she was thirty-four years old and we spoke eight years later.

• • •

I was to have a total hysterectomy, and it was during surgery that I had a cardiac arrest. The surgeon indicated that it was due to the anesthetic—he already knew that I'd had problems with anesthetics in previous operations. Anyway, at that time I became conscious of seeing my body lying there on the operating table, and I could hear the communication that was going on between the surgeon and the staff. I could see it all, but in a very detached sort of way. In an almost offhand way I realized that that was my body, and I realized that I'd died (in the physical sense). While I was in that out-of-body state I was aware of my husband and children so clearly, and yet there was no grief or sadness at the thought that I had died and was separate from them. I felt total peace, total rapture. There was no fear at all. And time didn't exist—it seemed like it was just a matter of a spit in time and I would be reunited with them anyway, so it wasn't an issue for me.

I then felt myself moving off very fast, exceedingly fast, into what seemed like outer space. I always felt that it was the fact of going so fast that gave me the sense of being in a tunnel. And I was going toward a very bright light. As I was traveling along I could see different-colored lights, and then I got stopped, just stopped before I got to the light. And I felt this extreme presence of love, just absolute love. It shocked me somewhat, but there was no problem with accepting that in essence I was being confronted with my creator.

I was also very conscious of communicating with other presences around me at that time, but I didn't see any. I was just conscious of so much love coming from those other presences as well. Then there was a review of my whole life. I can remember looking at it and assessing it and really judging it myself. I felt no one else judged me—I judged myself. I think the greatest shame I felt about my life was that I had totally rejected the concept of God. I'd totally given no acknowledgment to

God, I really didn't believe in God. And I felt such sadness, I was incredulous that I could ever have doubted that God existed, because He was so real and tangible—the whole essence of love. I say *He,* but that's just my conditioning. God was just this essence, this total essence of love.

At the time I felt the presence of that extreme love I could also hear beautiful music, wonderful music. I'm not sure if it was instrumental music, but somehow I think it was more massed voices giving that sound. But there were no words—it was more just a resonance of sound. And my consciousness seemed to increase dramatically, to the point where I felt all-knowing. I felt I was in touch with all knowledge—I just knew and understood so much more.

And the Light communicated with words. He said, "You'll now believe in me." He also said, "I made you a woman, I created you. I know everything about you and I'm now going to send you back, because it's not your time to come over. You still have your life's work to do." I felt very humble, very much in awe of such love. I could hardly believe that someone could love me so much.

At that time I remember asking what my life's work was, and I was told, "You'll not know at this time but you will be shown." And I think I was still asking questions like "When?" (laughs)—I was always saying, "When?" I was also told to come back and tell my husband and children what had happened. I was to share it with them. I think it was about then that I regained consciousness. I don't recall coming back. Strangely enough, I only recall waking up a day and a half later, and by that time I was back in the ward.

When I realized I was back in my body, I was a bit shattered that I couldn't be where I wanted to be. I didn't really want to be in my body, but at the same time I felt pretty good in that body. Almost immediately I noticed that there'd been a change in me. There was a complete change in my attitude to the people looking after me. I'd brought back with me a touch of that love and it stayed with me. And I think it's always remained—that sense of peace.

In the meantime my husband had realized just how seriously ill I was, and on the night of the operation, he'd gone home to have a shower and see to the children. He shares an experience that happened to him at that time. This was later to be relevant to both of us.

He was in the shower washing his hair, with his eyes closed. He was just feeling so dejected because he could see my face, like death, on the pillow, and he was consumed by grief. He felt that he was going to lose me. Suddenly he just felt his hand go up and found himself saying, "I believe, I believe, I believe." He didn't know why he did it—he was shocked at his movement. It was almost as though, on a higher level, his consciousness was acknowledging something. At that point he said he felt all the grief just lift off him, just like a blanket, and he had a conscious knowing that I was going to be all right. He didn't hear a voice, it was just a very real feeling. Then he called the hospital and heard that I'd stabilized, so he went to bed and slept the night.

The next morning he came to see me, and when I woke up he was there next to the bed. I said to him, "I died, didn't I?" At that stage he still hadn't spoken to the surgeon and he was quite startled to hear me say this. Not long after, the surgeon came in and said, "You're very lucky to be with us, we nearly lost you. We did lose you for a while." And I said, "Yes, I know. I died, didn't I?" And he said, "Yes, but how do you know?"

I explained to him what I'd seen and heard. He was

quite startled but he didn't say much. He just advised me never to have another operation that involved anesthetic, and told me I should always wear a disk.

I used to think you just died and that was it. But now I have no fear of death at all. I see it purely as a homecoming, it's just a total reunion, so much love and happiness. Intuitively I'm sure we go on and continue to keep learning. We continue to grow on another level.

I don't think I'd like to suicide, though, because it was very obvious to me that my endeavor to "go home" was premature, and I was told I had to come back. It was almost, "Come on, now, get back there and get on with it." But I do feel that if a person committed suicide, they would be met with total love and compassion, as I was. God is just total love.

I literally did have my life's work to do and I'd come to a state of acknowledging that we all do have a purpose in life. But it wasn't till eighteen months later that that purpose was made very clear to me. And that was a rather shattering experience.

At the time I was questioning what it had all been about. I knew I had a belief in a creator, and I knew there was a great purpose for us, but I didn't know what it was. I thought to myself, "I haven't changed my life so dramatically." We were just busily working in our dry-cleaning business, and living in a very comfortable suburban home that had all the usual equipment. But after [the NDE], all that was totally unimportant to me, so I kept saying, "Well, what's it all about? Did I have to come back just to do the same old thing?"

I had expressed that verbally to a friend. I'd said, "I really do believe in God, I have absolute faith that there is a purpose for us, but I don't relate to what the churches are telling us. I'm almost getting to the point of doubting that it even happened, because what's the point of it?'' So my logical mind was out there really chipping away at it, but it was not something I could share and talk about with many people.

Two days later I was standing there cooking, stirring a sauce, and being fairly introspective, and thinking, ''What is it, God, that you want me to do?'' At that point I just heard the same inner voice that I'd been confronted with when I left my body during the NDE. That presence of love came back and said, ''Pick up a pen and write down what you hear.'' I thought I was going crazy, but after the third time of hearing it—''Pick up the pen and write down what you hear''—I did it. And I started to ask questions: ''What is it we are to do?'' I was told that same afternoon that we were to go to the mountains in the south to make a place of rest and solace for many in the future.

After that it was incredible—every time I wanted to ask something, there was the answer. I knew it was coming from something external to myself, but within myself, if you can understand. I had answers of a spiritual depth that I knew wasn't me. And I really wondered how I was going to explain this to my husband and children. I shared it with Joe, and he believed me. Because he'd accepted what had happened to him in the shower, he knew there was a force looking after us, and he said, ''Well, let's find out what it is we have to do.'' So we kept asking questions, but all we could ever get was, ''Learn to be patient and you'll be shown the right place at the right time.''

There was this terrible tension in me to know what it was we had to do, and it was almost like an obsession for a few months. But of course that was my lesson—to learn patience and obedience. I had to learn to be led.

When we look at it now, it was exactly nine months, from that first time when I heard ''Pick up the pen and write,'' to when we actually moved here to Oakdale. It was the period of gestation. And for us it was a total rebirth in our lives. We changed our whole direction and mode of living.

But it was hard to talk about all this with others. I went to see two or three Protestant ministers and without failure they all said, "You shouldn't delve into things like that—you'll go mad, if you're not already mad. It's satanic and you're not meant to know about things like that. Just leave it aside." One of them did recommend I go seek psychiatric help. At that time it was so helpful to have Joe's support—he was very supportive. I *knew* that I wasn't going mad, I knew that there *was* total love. Then I talked to a Catholic priest quite by chance, just someone I met somewhere. He was no longer a priest, he'd left the church and was working as a Jungian analyst. He totally believed me and related to what I'd gone through. He said, "Look at mysticism, you're not odd. Just trust it, and just ask that you be protected and guarded." So that was like a ray of sunshine beaming in at a time when I was really starting to question whether or not there was maybe a problem.

I think of my experience as spiritual not religious. When I was young I was sent to the Methodist church. When I got into my teenage years I really questioned what it was all about and I stopped going. Now I would say I am spiritual. I have some problems with the word *religious. Religious* to me means someone who is steeped in dogma, whereas someone who is coming from a spiritual aspect is one who has had an actual experience of God. And it's been a very intimate experience with God, so therefore that person doesn't doubt God exists, and lives a life of example rather than preaches at people.

Today I find that my whole life is always a prayer to or a chat with God. I just talk to God like He's just there all the time. You know, if I need to know something, I'll just sit down and I'll tune in and ask what I should be doing. It's always there, that information. I meditate, too. For me the two can't be separated, because I think when I pray, I talk to God—just on that level of being close to a friend—and when I meditate, to me that's quietly listening. I just put myself into a quiet space and listen.

I've experienced many examples of psychic phenomena since my NDE. They usually take the form of guidance in some way or other. There was one particular example. We had been sitting in the garden, and Joe said to me, "I'd really like to go inside now. I'm really anxious to know a bit more about where we'll be going." We went inside and I got a pad. (I often found I had no retention of what I was hearing—it seemed to flow through me—so it was helpful to write it down.) Anyway, we were sitting on the internal staircase and Joe was sitting on a stair below me. I went within myself and I was praying. I asked for protection, as I always did, and I virtually expressed what it was that I wanted to know. I was sitting there with my eyes closed. Suddenly this energy came into me. I thought first off I was having a heart attack, because I could feel this incredible energy come into where my heart area is, and it was spiraling. But then I thought, "This isn't pain, this is rapture, absolute rapture." I had my eyes closed, but I could see right in front of me this bright light again. Joe said the tears were just streaming down my cheeks.

In his mind he heard, "Put your head on Janet's shoulder." When he did he felt the energy flow right into his body, and at that point he saw the light, and we both heard a message, "You are as my disciples and I have chosen you to go and do this work," and there was this incredible feeling of love. We then realized that it was in answer to the fact that we were allowing our logical minds to doubt the guidance. And I said, "I'll never doubt again." How could I have doubted again! I thought, "I've doubted God all over again!" After my

NDE I never thought I'd doubt again. But it wasn't until we had the most amazing experience of all that we stopped doubting.

Only a matter of a few months later it happened. It all first started happening when I picked up that pen. I was getting clearer in my guidance. Whenever I asked where was the place, it just said, "Don't worry about a thing, you'll know soon enough."

I said, "I need some help with my doubting."

It said, "Don't worry, it will all be different after you've seen the play."

And I was asking, "What play?"

"It's a play with a man in it with a mustache, by the name of William, and there's also another man, who's a man of God, and he will have a message for you which will change your whole life."

Up to that time it had been fairly elevated spiritual guidance, and here I was getting this kooky sort of stuff. I shared it with Joe and he looked at me a bit strangely, too, but everytime I asked, I got, "Wait till you've seen the play."

One morning I was serving a customer and she said, "I've just opened a play, you must come." I thought I should check with Joe, and so I went on with serving someone else. As she walked out of the shop I heard so clearly, "Go and get the tickets!" So off I went. The play was called *The Ballad of Billy Lane.*

Later I was at home, in the kitchen washing a lettuce, and I heard clearly in my mind, "Go downstairs, Joe wants you." I thought, "Oh, what now?" because some months earlier I'd been told intuitively to go downstairs, and when I got there, I could see Joe drilling through our bedroom wall—he was drilling through the back of a double power point and was about to electrocute himself! So here I was rushing downstairs, and when I got down, he called me and said, "Come here and have a look at my hands." He was just washing his hands under the tap, and I looked at his hands and they were a really unusual color—they'd gone a deep, browny color, and all the little veins and sinews were standing out. It was like looking through a high-powered magnifying glass. I just looked in amazement. Mine were perfectly normal. Then I just felt as though someone standing next to me gently took hold of my right hand and looked at it and put it under Joe's hand. We both heard the same thing: "Don't look at your hands, look at Joe's." Well, we both had goose bumps by this time, and his hands returned to normal, before our eyes, and we just cuddled each other and we said, "What on earth is this all about?" And we just asked that we'd have some understanding of what it was all about. We didn't have any idea.

I don't remember driving to the theater because all we could talk about was, "What on earth is going on?" We got to the theater right at curtain time and they handed me a program as we rushed to our seats. As I opened the program I said to Joe, "You won't believe this, but this play's about a man called William." He said, "Look, we've had enough excitement for one night—can't we just come to a theater like normal people?" And I said, "But I'm sure this is the play. Can you feel the energy in the place. It's just so full of more than just the people here." I could feel something was going on, and I've said since then that God's got a wonderful sense of humor, and he sold tickets so that people could come and see our faces.

Anyway, we were sitting there watching this play, and it starts with singing, and the man's got this huge handlebar mustache. It's a true story. William Lane heard a voice—he wanted to go and set up a new place, which he did. And he was talking to people: "We'll do it through sharing, and brotherly love and caring about each other." And out into this window box above the stage came someone dressed as a priest depicted as a guardian angel, and he said, ''You'll fail, Billy—you're leaving God out of it.'' By this time we were both listening. As it turned out, it did fail and the priest came out again and said, ''I told you you'd fail, Billy—you left God out of it.''

In essence he was setting up a community very similar to what we were being told to do. William got really angry and said, ''Go and get out of my mind. You know I don't even believe in God. I can do it, I don't need you.'' And the priest said, ''How can you not believe in God, who created you? Look at the universe, look at the planets, and look at the stars. Look at nature, look at a leaf, look at a flower, and look at the beauty of it all.'' And then he boomed out to Billy, ''Look at your own hands! Look at the color, look at the lines, look at the veins, look at the sinews! Who do you think made them?'' By then Joe was almost under the seat. At that point, Billy picked his fist up and said, ''I believe, I believe, I believe.'' Now it was almost like the night Joe was in the shower.

The whole thing brought up all sorts of stuff for us, as you can imagine. I think we walked out of the theater, I don't know. We went into the park next door to the theater, and stood and looked up at the sky, and we just said, ''All right, God, we're prepared to listen. We realize now that you are talking to us.'' And that was our definite one-hundred-percent proof. We knew that it solved something for us, because we knew there was no logical reason why I could have been told about something that came out of an actor's mouth on the stage—and it was all preplanned. And when we shared what'd happened with the actress friend, she said that the whole cast had been affected in doing that play. They felt they were being overlighted in what they did, and they got us to come back and talk to the cast about that experience. So that was the big clincher for us that made us commit our lives totally.

That night when we got home from the play, I'd had a bad throat. I said, "If God can move mountains to draw our attention, surely he can fix this silly throat of mine." (Little did I realize, I later read a book by Edgar Cayce which told how he got a sore throat whenever he was not trusting.) And I said, "Do you think I could ask for some healing for my throat?" Joe came and put his hands on my shoulders and was sort of saying a prayer: "God, can you fix Janet's throat?" He felt one of his hands go above my head, inscribe a circle, and then he felt it come right down until it was about six inches above my head. All he was aware of was this intense pressure that was there, and he didn't understand what was going on. At that point, I lifted off out of my body, just like in my NDE, and I actually flew up this valley, and saw this huge cliff face, and I was thinking all sorts of things like, "What am I being shown?" Then I saw the eucalyptus trees, then I saw these oak trees down here near the river, and I knew they weren't Australian, so I was fairly confused what it was about. And just when I started to get really afraid of it—"How am I going to get back in my body?"—I was, *zoom,* back in. As soon as the fear set in, that limited the whole experience, and I was back in my body really fast. And I said to Joe, "I don't know where this place is, but I'm sure I've just been shown the place we're going to." It wasn't till November that the guidance told us it was up in the mountains near Tumut. We were told it would be close to Tumut yet remote, and we were told it was a very beautiful place. When we came to Tumut on Boxing Day of 1982, we just followed our guidance and that was another whole series of miracles.

It was all to get us to the point where we were doing our lifework. I now feel that my whole life is totally guided by God. My life has totally changed—I am doing things now that I never dreamed I could do as a result of the work we're doing here. I was terribly shy, but now I just know that it's not a worry to talk about [the experience]—I know I've experienced it, so I'm an expert at it, I can speak from the heart.

And my relationship with Joe has really strengthened through the NDE—I think because of the fact that we both became aware that we had a job to do. Our children accepted it very well, too. We lost a lot of friends for a while there, because they thought we'd gone religious or something, until they found that we weren't really out there Bible-bashing or going to church, but we were living something that they were quite amazed about. . . . So, interestingly, a lot of our older friends who thought we had gone a bit funny at first, are now gradually coming back. And they are actually quite interested in what we do.

We've virtually reached the stage now, we were told by inner guidance, that we had to teach by example and we were to be teaching what faith in God could do. We were asked to give up personal income, so Oakdale functions on donations—it's a nonprofit center. We've made it into a trust, we've handed it all over so we don't own it anymore. We were told not to have any income, but we were to take whatever Oakdale could afford to pay us, if and when. And now for the last twelve months we've lived that way and that was pretty scary at first. I went through tantrums and told God off over that one. And here we are twelve months later, and all has been flowing just so smoothly and all our needs are met abundantly, and I realize that we're having to do it purely as an example to show people that there is a power beyond ourselves that is controlling and planning. To me it was a case of total surrender and total freedom.

My main interest today is in developing Oakdale. I have the sense that our life is an act of service now. We are to give out as much as we can to humanity in order hopefully to bring about a change.

We're practically vegetarian now—it's been a gradual thing for us. And we've been told that we have to put more nut trees and fruit trees in the garden, to plan for the future. We need more pairs of hands to help put the gardens in, but I think they'll come once the buildings are up.

I think that really our whole lifestyle is just being totally conscious of the need to live the very best way we know how—not to abuse our bodies. Also in our relationship with people, we really got the message that we had to forgive everyone we had any grievance against—whether or not they chose to accept it, it still had to be put right.

I'm concerned about our earth. Therefore we've made Oakdale into a wildlife sanctuary and endeavor to do everything organically. We try not to pollute our earth any further in our own lives. So we're talking as much as we can to all the people who come here to try to raise their consciousnesses as to what's going on.

I'm not working for the peace movement, but I think, on the level of inner peace, I'm working full speed ahead, because that's where I believe it really stems from. If you can get people to really acknowledge that sense of needing to be totally at one and at peace with God and themselves, then obviously that has to flow out into the universe.

Afterword

I now feel that my life is totally guided by God. . . . To me it was a case of total surrender and total freedom.
—Janet

After reading these twenty stories it must now be apparent that the near-death experience acts as a powerful catalyst for change in the lives of experiencers. The forms these changes take may differ from person to person, but taken as a whole, there is a definite underlying pattern, almost as obvious as the underlying pattern of the experience itself.

NDErs have *no* fear of death, and their heightened spiritual awareness and enhanced intuition suffuse much of their interaction in the social world. NDErs themselves consider this growth in spirituality and love, and their sense of having an ongoing relationship with God, or the Light, or a Higher Power, to be the most significant of these changes, and the source of the profound transformation in their lives. They *know* from their own experience what it is to be unconditionally loved. They know what it is to be guided and looked after in their daily lives. And although it is sometimes easy to forget when overtaken by everyday stresses, they *know* at a deep level that they have been, and are still, one with the Light.

But this understanding is not for near-death experiencers alone. It is an insight to be shared with all humanity. In their own lives NDErs struggle with this knowledge. By reading their accounts, by speaking with them and by truly *hearing* what they have to tell us, we can all participate in this process. Not only do they teach us that death is a homecoming, a reunion in love and light, they also teach us that that love and that light are already here in our lives. As Moira said:

> *We are all a part of God. We are immersed in spirit . . . but we don't recognize it because we have this sense of separation. But once we can get over the sense of separation we'll know who we really are and then we'll be able to start expressing it.*

That is, in the present, we are already within the light and the light is already within us. We only need to lower our barriers to see that this is so. It is this recognition and its corollary, as Anthea said, that "everything is so intricate, and so valuable and so beautiful," that has the potential to make such a difference to our planet. In Janet's words:

> *If people can really acknowledge that sense of needing to be totally at one and at peace with God and themselves, then obviously that has to flow out into the universe.*

Endnotes

Full details can be found in the Selected Bibliography.

Preface

1. AUSTRALIANDS is the Australian chapter of IANDS, the International Association for Near-Death Studies.
   Address: AUSTRALIANDS, P.O. Box 493, Vaucluse, NSW 2030, Australia.

Introduction

1. Gallup, *Adventures in Immortality.*
2. Sabom, *Recollections of Death,* p. 57.

Chapter 1

1. See especially, Morse, *Closer to the Light.*
2. Serdahely, pp. 219-24.

Chapter 2

1. Moody, *Life After Life,* p. 143.
2. Moody, *Reflections on Life After Life,* pp. 43-9.
3. Ring, *Life at Death,* p. 119.
4. Ring, *Heading Toward Omega,* p. 45.
5. For more detail on Kate's story, see Sutherland, *Reborn in the Light.*
6. See Sutherland, *Reborn in the Light,* pp. 86-8.
7. Moody, *The Light Beyond,* p. 40.
8. The ability to hear things not present to the senses.

Chapter 3

1. See Zaleski.
2. Plato, *The Republic,* pp. 393-6.
3. Moody, *Reflections on Life After Life,* p. 36.
4. Ring, *Life at Death,* pp. 192-6.
5. See *The Bible,* Deuteronomy 33:27 "The eternal God is thy refuge, and underneath are the everlasting arms."

Chapter 4

1. For more detail on my NDE, see Preface to Sutherland, *Reborn in the Light.*
2. For more detail on Hal's story, see Sutherland, *Reborn in the Light,* and Elder, *And When I Die Will I Be Dead?*

3. For more detail on Martine's story, see Sutherland, *Reborn in the Light.*
4. The "otherworld bridge" is a common motif in medieval accounts also. (See Zaleski.)
5. Thanks are due to Takeshi Tachibana for his generosity in sharing these two experiences with me.

Chapter 5

1. For more detail on Helen's story, see Sutherland, *Reborn in the Light.*
2. Ring, *Heading Toward Omega,* p. 74.
3. See Allen for more detail on this experience.

Selected Bibliography

Allen, J. "Transformation," *AUSTRALIANDS,* 4:2 (1993).

Atwater, P.M.H. "Is There a Hell? Surprising Observations About the Near-Death Experience," *Journal of Near-Death Studies,* 10:3 (1992), 149-60.

Elder, B. *And When I Die Will I Be Dead?* Sydney: ABC, 1987.

Gallup, G. *Adventures in Immortality.* U.K.: Souvenir Press, 1983.

Grey, M. *Return from Death.* London: Arkana, 1985.

Greyson, B. and Evans-Bush, N. "Distressing Near-Death Experiences," *Psychiatry,* 55 (1992), 95-110.

Moody, R. A. Jr. *Life After Life.* New York: Bantam Books, 1975.

Moody, R. A. Jr. *Reflections on Life After Life.* New York: Bantam Books, 1983 (first published 1977).

Moody, R. A. Jr. *The Light Beyond.* New York: Bantam Books, 1988.

Morse, M. *Closer to the Light.* New York: Villard Books, 1990.

Plato. *The Republic.* Harmondsworth, U.K.: Penguin, 1973.

Rawlings, M. *Beyond Death's Door.* Sydney: Bantam Books, 1981 (first published 1978).

Ring, K. *Life at Death.* New York: Coward, McCann & Geoghan, 1980.

Ring, K. *Heading Toward Omega,* New York: William Morrow & Co. Inc., 1984.

Sabom, M. B. *Recollections of Death.* New York: Harper & Row, 1982.

Serdahely, W. J. "A Comparison of Retrospective Accounts of Childhood Near-Death Experiences with Contemporary Pediatric Near-Death Experience Accounts, *Journal of Near-Death Studies,* 9:4 (1991). 219-24.

Sutherland, C. *Reborn in the Light.* New York: Bantam Books, 1995.

Zaleski, C. *Otherworld Journeys: Accounts of Near-Death Experience in Medieval and Modern Times.* Oxford U.K.: Oxford University Press, 1987.

Useful Addresses

AUSTRALIANDS (Australian chapter of the International Association for Near-Death Studies)
P.O. Box 493
Vaucluse
NSW 2030
Australia

IANDS (International Association for Near-Death Studies)
P.O. Box 502
East Windsor Hill
CT 06028
USA

Index

About the Author

DR. CHERIE SUTHERLAND, who has had a near-death experience herself, is a Visiting Research Fellow in the School of Sociology at the University of New South Wales. Since beginning her near-death research, she has lectured widely on the subject and been involved in several film projects. She is currently engaged in research for a book on the death of children, which will include further consideration of childhood near-death experiences.

If you were intrigued by WITHIN THE LIGHT, you'll be fascinated by Dr. Cherie Sutherland's REBORN IN THE LIGHT.

Read on for a sample . . .

Preface

Eden, my youngest son, was born on January 11, 1971. The inspired irony of my having given him such a name did not occur to me until reading Ken Wilber's book *Up From Eden* many years later. Certainly the evolution of my life moved "up" from the time of Eden's birth—if not precisely as Ken Wilber outlines. Rather than it being a movement from Eden to self-consciousness, I moved at the time of the experience, during the birth of Eden, to self-consciousness. For however long it was, I experienced the essence of who I am: selfless, egoless, bodyless, free of time and space.

This experience, which even at the time I recognized as one of death and rebirth, was to provide me with a view of reality and a consciousness of self that I had not even imagined to be a possibility, and was profoundly to alter my life.

During Eden's birth I passed from a physical experience of great pain and fear to another realm quite free of any physical discomfort—a realm of peace, calm and love. The ineffability of such an experience has often been noted. To reduce to words an experience so far removed from the construct of reality within which I had previously lived is inevitably to oversimplify and do it violence. However, in brief, I found that I was moving very quickly through a dark tunnel toward a magnificent bright light, hearing a "whooshing" sound as I went. As I approached the light, it became brighter and I saw that it was like very bright but gentle sunlight. I could see into the light where everything was bathed in a golden glow. There were gently rolling fields, flowers, an extraordinarily beautiful sight . . . joyous and peaceful. However, I stopped just short of the light, still in the tunnel. I knew I had a choice: to go on (and it was very tempting) or to go back. I reflected with great clarity that the baby I was giving birth to needed me, and my other son (still very young) also needed me, so I would go back. In addition to going back for the sake of my babies, however, I knew I was going back for me—that I would have another go at life. Once the decision was made, I found that I was traveling backward back down the tunnel away from the light and was returned to the pain of my immediate situation—giving birth to Eden.

As soon as I found out, to have experienced this transcendental state did not mean that I was to be freed of my ego-bound self. The gift of this experience was to leave me with the direct knowledge that my ego-bound self was and is a part of the timeless ground of all being, integral wholeness. As Kenneth Ring notes in *Life at Death*, it is this direct knowledge that has "core near-death experiencers" (and mystics generally) speaking with such certitude about their experiences, whereas those who haven't had such direct experience are often left feeling skeptical or just indifferent.

A year later I told my mother about the experience. She was somewhat distressed, but accepting of its reality. Any later attempts I made to talk about my experience were generally greeted with skepticism. Rational, materialistic, reductionistic explanations were even "helpfully" offered to "get rid of it" for me. So, I stopped talking about it. Yet I had no doubt that it was important for me. From being fearful of everything, I now found within myself a realization that there was nothing to fear. As Ken Wilber writes in *Up From Eden*:

> Seeing that self and other are one, [we are] released from the fear of life; seeing that being and non-being are one, [we are] delivered from the fear of death.[1]

In this present study I have found that people are greatly changed by such experiences in terms of personal renewal—given new direction, purpose and energy. I certainly was. From my social situation as an uneducated housebound housewife, mother of two young sons, I began to make what now seem rather tentative forays into the world, but at the time seemed like giant risk-taking steps. I began to learn yoga and practiced it daily with my babies. I began to read about vegetarianism and practiced it from then on. I read anything I could lay my hands on, and, as time passed, began painting and writing. In essence, I continued to learn through valuing my own experience—a theme that has evolved over the years as a central concern of my own development. Further, against all expectations, synchronistically, university fees were abolished the year Eden was old enough to attend preschool and my application to college was accepted.

The experience I have so briefly outlined thus was to provide the starting point for my doctoral thesis and this book. It has remained to this day the source to which I return and from which I continue to learn so much. As Ken Wilber writes:

> I used to think that one adopted a path just to get to a goal. I have learned better. The true path is itself the ultimate goal.[2]

CHAPTER 1

The Near-Death Experience

There is a general assumption in modern Western society that death is final, that it is as Shakespeare described it in *Hamlet*: ‘‘The undiscover’d country from whose bourn, No traveller returns, . . .’’ Yet there have always been tales of people who have returned, to tell of realms unknown. In literature of all ages there are accounts of such journeys. Plato, in *The Republic*, recounts the story of Er, a Greek soldier killed in battle, whose body revived twelve days later on the funeral pyre. To the surprise of all present, he described the journey his soul had taken until ordered to return. In the many centuries of medieval literature, Christian ‘‘otherworld’’ accounts abound. For example, in the eighth century, the Venerable Bede relates the story of the vision of Drythelm, a devoute Northumbrian man who died one night after a severe illness. To the amazement of all those weeping around the body, he revived suddenly the next day. He reassured his wife: ‘‘Do not be afraid, for I have indeed risen from death which held me in its bonds, and I have been permitted to live again amongst mankind; nevertheless after this I must not live as I used to, but in a very different way."[1]

Such experiences are also described in other religious and cultural traditions. For example, the theories of the Tibetan *Bardo Thodol*, or *Book of the Dead*, which are now well known in the West, describe the journey of the disembodied individual from the moment of death through the after-death states. There are many similarities between modern accounts and descriptions of Japanese death-bed visions and the Bahá'í faith's account of the afterlife Kingdom of Light. Carl Becker argues that the near-death experience is also central to Chinese Pure-Land Buddhism, and E. J. Hermann reveals that there is a strong affinity between the beliefs of near-death experiencers and those of Taoist patriarch Chuang Tzu.

In the late nineteenth century, Swiss geologist Albert Heim, having survived death himself in a mountain-climbing accident, published his collection of accounts by fellow climbers who had also survived near-fatal falls. At the same time, especially in Britain and the United States, pioneer psychic researchers had become fascinated by the tantalizing possibility of finding a proof for "survival." They scrutinized such phenomena as apparitions seen by a number of people, mediumistic messages from the dead, out-of-body experiences, and visions described by the dying. In 1926 Sir William Barrett published his collection of "death-bed vision" case studies, which was to become the classic work on that topic. Some thirty-five years later, Carl Gustav Jung, in his autobiographical work, *Memories, Dreams, Reflections*, described his own intense, life-changing vision precipitated by a heart attack in 1944.

In more recent times, with advances in modern resuscitation technology, even more people have been brought back from the brink of death to recount their experiences. However, it was not until 1975, with the publication of Raymond Moody's *Life After Life*, that there was a more general resurgence of interest in the phenomenon he was to name the near-death experience.

The near-death experience is said to occur when a person is close to death (or in many cases actually clinically dead), and yet is resuscitated or somehow survives to recount an intense, profoundly meaningful experience. The near-death episode itself is typically characterized by a feeling of peace, an out-of-body experience, the sensation of traveling very quickly through a dark tunnel, generally toward a light, an encounter with the spirits of deceased relatives or friends or a "being of light," an instantaneous life review and for some, entrance into a world of light.

In 1983 a major survey by George Gallup, Jr., reported that eight million Americans, or approximately five percent of the adult American population, had had what he calls a "verge-of-death" or "temporary death" experience with some sort of mystical encounter associated with the actual death event. In 1989 an Australian survey by Allan Kellehear and Patrick Heaven found that ten percent of a sample of 173 people, when shown a vignette depicting five typical elements of a near-death experience, claimed to have had a similar experience. In a prospective hospital study in the United States, Michael Sabom found that forty-three percent reported a near-death experience following a near-death crisis. If so many people are having this experience and if, as Drythelm suggested so long ago, their values, beliefs and life practices are indeed changed by it, this phenomenon is of considerable interest and significance.

The empirical work that has been done in this area has been carried out mostly in America during the last fifteen years and has been predominantly psychological or medical in focus. Raymond Moody, in his popular first book *Life After Life*, provided an ideal or composite picture of the near-death experience that he maintained contained all the common elements of the experience. The current study, although confirming the presence of most of those elements, uncovered a pattern more in accord with that found by Kenneth Ring in his scientific investigation of the phenomenon reported in *Life at Death*. Ring observed that in his own examination of near-death experiences, the core experience unfolds in stages, with the earlier stages being far more common than the latter. The stages are:

Peace and the sense of well-being
Body separation: leaving the body behind
Entering the darkness
Seeing the light
Entering the light

So, what is this phenomenon? How is it described by the near-death experiencers themselves?

Overwhelmingly the experience is characterized by its ineffability. Although people do in fact manage to give some sort of description, they often stress that their words can in no way do it justice or convey its awesome power. A young woman who had her experience at age sixteen during an operation for cancer of the thyroid, while trying to explain the noise she heard, said:

> It was sort of like silvery moonbeams and the noise they'd make on water if they were going to make a noise. You know what I mean? A sort of brushing sound.

Later she remarked:

> That's the problem I'm having, when I put it into an intellectual frame of mind, when I try to write it out on a bit of paper. I'd say well, it wasn't actually this head thinking it. It was something dif-

ferent, totally devoid of intellectualization, totally devoid of the little boxes that we put things into.

Peace and Well-being

All of my samples, in one way or another, described a feeling of peace and well-being. A man who as a sixteen-year-old schoolboy, undiagnosed, entered a diabetic coma remembered:

> I had an intense feeling of well-being which for me created a really strong impression because I'd never felt that. I'd never had that feeling. Since though, sometimes in meditation I've touched upon it but then I've messed it up by grasping at it too strongly. There is an intense craving to get back to that feeling.

Another woman, who at ten years of age was suffering from double pneumonia and was not expected to survive the night, remembered:

> I was floating on the ceiling and I was just so, so happy. It was just complete happiness, just complete happiness. There really is no word to describe it, there really isn't. And even now all those years later I get very overwhelmed at the feeling.

Leaving the Body Behind

Movement out of body is often the first indication that something is amiss. In general, the experience is for people to find themselves looking down on their bodies as spectator, often from a vantage point near the ceiling (as described in the previous example). They usually report that at the time it all seems perfectly natural.

A thirty-six-year-old woman had a massive hemorrhage after a home birth. She described the scene below her:

> I sort of sat up on the ceiling. I remember watching all the panic, total panic. Tina, the midwife, couldn't find a pulse, she couldn't get a needle in. I was bleeding. I couldn't work out why everyone was so fussed. I was interested when Tina said "the veins have gone flat." Then I was aware that another friend there, whose mother had just died three months before, she was really frightened. But I felt an incredible feeling of peace . . . At one stage they were looking for elastic to make a tourniquet so they could get a vein, and I knew where it was. In the end I said where it was but they didn't hear me.

Another experiencer, a man who at fourteen had had a series of heart attacks while at school one day, recalled attempting to communicate with the people around his body and generally exploring his immediate environment:

> I was up above everything. I could still hear them talking and by that time there were six teachers there. I was out of my body and I thought to myself "I must be dead." So I went up to Miss Smith and told her not to bother, I was dead. She took no notice of me. I went to take her arm and my hand went right through her. I thought, something is very wrong here! I made a few more attempts to speak to her and to Miss Breen, then I gave up. I went to open the door but my hand went through the handle. I then tried the bricks beside the door,

> pushed with my hand and then went straight through the bricks to the outside. I remember going through the bricks two or three times just to try it out. I noticed some girls playing hockey. Then I started to wonder where my body was and somehow or other I got back into my body.

Entering the Darkness and Seeing the Light

Many words have been used to describe the experience of entering the darkness. It has variously been spoken of as a channel, a valley, a trough, a void or a pipe, but most commonly it is described as a tunnel.

A twenty-seven-year-old woman who was rushed by ambulance from a country town to a city hospital with a burst appendix during pregnancy experienced the darkness as "a valley, a dark valley, with this light sort of figure coming toward me."

Another woman who was hospitalized while hemorrhaging during a miscarriage at six months remembered:

> . . . falling down this huge, huge, huge, big tunnel or at the time, because it's falling, you feel like it's a pit, a well, a bottomless well. And you feel as if it's bottomless and you feel as if it's a well but I suppose it's like falling down a big tunnel.

As can already be seen, however convenient it might be to break up and talk about the experience in terms of common elements or stages, this is not the way it is experienced by those describing it. Although these patterns become obvious when examining the reports of a large number of people, each individual case is unique and is experienced as a whole, not as a series of discrete parts.

The Life Review

A woman who, aged twenty-nine, had her experience during an operation for a tubal ligation, described a "life review," entering the darkness, and seeing the light. She said:

> I went into this kind of feeling of ecstasy and just started moving outward energetically. . . . And then I experienced a replay of all of my life and I'd love to know if other people have it. That was the most shocking thing of the whole experience, from my birth to the actual operation. I actually felt the operation. And it was like it was on fast-forward video. I didn't even know about videos at the time but I know in recalling it. And it was through everything, every single thing that had ever happened. It was just the most amazing experience. And people, places, everything. I re-experienced my whole life. . . . Straight after that I started . . . the darkness. I could see a light—it was like a light I could never describe—like a silver-white light. . . . It was just massive darkness and then massive light. I felt myself, just my being, move toward that, and just about three quarters of the way in the darkness and the light was beyond that, then they filled my lungs with air. I didn't even know that was going on—and suddenly I took this breath and I was back. And that was extremely shocking.

Spiritual Contact

Many people hear the voice, or note the presence, of spiritual beings at some point during their experience. These are generally deceased relatives or friends. The man who attempted suicide, aged thirty-two, described moving toward the light, when a voice told him to go back. He said:

> As I got very close to it I heard a voice distinctly sing out, a very strong voice: "Go back!" really loud, but not scary, not angry. And I thought, well, that's what I'll do. I think when I look at it now I was on the edge, nearly there. Then I just started to slide back, slowly slide back. By this time, I didn't know, but my sister had arrived and there was an old priest, I couldn't believe it, anointing me with the last rites.

Another woman, who had a cardiac arrest during a hysterectomy, remembered:

> I was going toward a very bright light. And as I was traveling along I could see different colored lights and then I got stopped, just stopped before I got to the light. And I felt this extreme presence of love, just absolute love. And I heard very clearly. . . . It shocked me somewhat but there was no problem with accepting that in essence I was being confronted with my creator. At that time I felt the presence of that extreme love but also I could hear beautiful music, wonderful music. My consciousness seemed to increase dramatically as though I just knew and understood so much more. I was told it wasn't my time to go on, that I had to come back, I had my life's work to do. At that time I remember asking what my life's work was. And I was told, you'll not know at this time but you will be shown. And I think I was still asking questions like "When?" I was always saying "When?" I was also told to come back and to tell my husband and children.

In another case, a woman remembered the experience she had as a seven-year-old child when, critically ill with pneumonia, she was left at home with her mother—the expectation being that she would die during the day.

> I saw this lovely white stairway with a lot of blue around it, kind of misty, cloudy, and I saw this lovely lady coming down the stairs in a long white robe, and she had a beautiful face and I recognized her instantly. It makes me go goose bumps just to think of it even now. And, anyhow, she said, "Don't be afraid, Jennifer." And I said, "I'm not afraid, Great-grandmother." She said: "You know me?" And I said, "Yes, Great-grandmother." And she said: "Take my hand, I've come to show you the way." And she stretched out her hand to me. And I said: "Oh, I'd love to come with you, Great-grandmother, but I can't go now because Mom needs me and she's got no one to look after her but me."

Entering the Light

Some people actually entered the light. A woman who was in a difficult labor when she lost consciousness described what she experienced:

> Suddenly I found myself in a place, it was a real place. . . . It was like, there were gently rolling hills, no crags, nor sharp edges, nothing that was cruel, nothing that was other than gentle. The sky was intense blue, the scene was gently rolling, I know you've heard this before but that's what it was. And there seemed to be figures, grouped, almost a theatrical grouping, like a stage set. . . . And as I looked, one of the figures seemed to re-

solve itself, and I looked and I thought, oh God, it's my Aunty Hannah, who died eleven years ago, and then I saw my Uncle Abraham, who died before I was born, and I knew them. . . . They knew me even though they'd never met me. I'm going to end up crying. My granny, who I'd never met, my grandfather, just all the people I've never known and those I had known who'd died many years before, or who'd even died recently . . . Anyway, then I turned and I looked at this figure standing next to me—it was my father. My dad died when I was sixteen. . . . Dad spoke to me although there was no speaking, his mind spoke to me. And he said, "No, honey, you're not imagining, it's not coming from you, you're with me and this is our time to talk." Anyway, we talked, laid the ghosts to rest. . . . And I looked down and there was my dog, Lucky. He died when I was very young, and he was just there. Sounds crazy, doesn't it? . . . And then there was a sense of drawing back, and I panicked and I said, "Dad, I don't want to go!" He said: "You have to go, you must go back, you're going to have a son, and you have to bring this boy up, bring him up by yourself." I said: "Dad I don't want to go. I want to stay with you." I was most distressed, I didn't want to go back. He sent me back . . . and I seemed to be moving back quickly, like, there was no sense of travel, but just I was there . . . I was there in the delivery room again and I was crying. My husband was allowed back in and I was sobbing and sobbing and I was exhausted. I was sobbing with the tears running down my cheeks and I said: "I was just with my dad." John said: "You're just imagining things."

As these examples show, some people are told to come back, while others are given the choice. Some decide to return, for their children, their parents or for whatever reason, and others just suddenly find themselves back in their bodies. Most people do not remember actually getting back into their bodies, although one of my sample, a twenty-nine-year-old who had an NDE as a result of a bloodstream infection following the removal of a kidney, said: ''Immediately I was back in my body, fully. It was just like somebody pushed me back in there . . . and I do remember waking up in agonizing pain.''

One element that appears to be almost universal in near-death accounts is the difficulty near-death experiencers have in talking about the experience afterward. It needs to be emphasized that this is not just because of their inability to describe the experience fully, although of course what is known is so different from normal ''knowing'' that it is almost impossible to describe to someone who has not encountered it. There is also a reluctance to describe such events, which stems from experiencers' perception of social attitudes to these phenomena. This comes from a fear of being laughed at, hushed up, thought crazy or simply presumed to be lying. A determined silence is often the result.

Response to the near-death experience has in fact been varied. Some see it as providing evidence for an afterlife, a goal earnestly sought by psychic researchers for over a century. Others take what Osis and Haraldsson so eloquently call a position of ''tactical agnosticism,'' by which they mean that researchers deny near-death experiences can provide evidence for an afterlife, yet admit that they personally, and most of their interviewees, are convinced of it. There have also been a number of attempts at explanation that have offered physiological, pharmacological and psychological means to explain away the phenomenon. Some of these are the result not of science but "scientism." As Huston Smith writes, scientism "goes beyond the actual findings of science to deny that other approaches to knowledge are valid and other truths true."[2] Close scrutiny of the reductionistic arguments offered so far has found them less than convincing.

Although the phenomenology of the near-death experience is of intrinsic interest, it is now well recorded and well established. This study notes details of experiences by a sample of Australians, but these are examined only insofar as they form a context for the personal and social process of life after near-death experience. My starting point is that the near-death experience exists, that it is real in the minds of those who have had it and, in particular, that it is real in its consequences. This book examines these consequences.